*instant***EXPERT**

COLLECTING QUILTS

ANNE GILBERT

Alliance Publishers, Inc.

ISBN 1-887110-06-2

Design by Cynthia Dunne

Lonestar or Texas Quilt.
Courtesy of Kavanagh's Antiques, FL

Pieced concentric Square. c1920.
Courtesy of Textile Conservators, Inc., Chicago IL

Alliance Publishers, Inc.
P. O. Box 080377
Brooklyn, New York 11208-0002

Distributed to the trade by National Book Network, Inc.

10 8 6 4 2 1 3 5 7 9

ACKNOWLEDGMENTS

Just as quilts require many pieces and talented hands to put them together in an artful way, so does a book on the subject. My deep appreciation goes to collector Amy Goodhart who shared her knowledge and allowed me to educate my camera's eye to the wonders of fine quilting. To collector/quilt maker Patty Trevarthen who alerted me to the many quilt-making groups around the country and to Sandy Mason, whose interest in quilts led to both a quilt-making business, and a revival of interest in quilting, my sincere thanks for their input. A special thanks to specialist dealers like Laura Fisher and Linda Reuther who took the time to discuss the current quilt market. And, to Skinner Galleries, Leslie Hindman Auctioneers, and Sotheby's, the auction galleries that influence the quilt market, for their photographs and interviews with their experts, much thanks.

Thanks to Art Quilt artists Jane Sassaman, Judith Perry, and Marcia Karlin who are proof that quilts are an art form.

For background material on contemporary quilters and quilting, much thanks to Pamela Lewis of Quilts Inc., International Quilt Festival and Hilary M. Fletcher, Project Director, the Dairy Barn Southeastern Ohio Cultural Arts Center, sponsors of Quilt National.

To Dorothy Harris, who always seems to have "another book" for me to write. "You can do it," she says. And, with her encouragement I somehow do. Thanks for nudging me into unfamiliar places.

CONTENTS

When I was asked to do this book, my first thought was to gather material on old, traditional quilts. But, the more I researched, the more it became increasingly clear that beginning in the twentieth century, quilts and quilt making had evolved and taken on different forms. Today, new techniques, materials, and technologies have and are changing the look of quilts and the way we view them.

I also discovered that quilts made from 1900 thru the 1950s are being seriously collected, with an eye to the future. Even if the 1950s seem unlikely, consider that there was a major crafts revival after World War II...that included quilts. I also learned that the stylized designs of the 60s and 70s were adapted to quilting. It just goes on and on.

Now, it's the 90s and once again there is a great resurgence in making and collecting quilts. While traditional patterns are still a favorite, from a collector's standpoint, it is the emergence of the Art quilt that offers the most exciting potential. But, would they be of interest to the quilt collector or the art collector? You will have to decide. While traditional antique quilts are being displayed in various ways, it is only the Art quilt that is designed specifically to be hung or otherwise shown as art.

The purpose of this book is not only to offer a selection of quilts and brief evaluations, but also to stimulate your interest and open your mind to the many wondrous possibilities. There are also related items, such as pattern kits that can be included in your collection. Whether you make them or collect them, the quilts you own will become the treasured family heirlooms of future generations.

As our technology becomes ever more sophisticated, the individual handwork of quilt makers could become a thing of the past. This makes the continuing work of the quilt maker and the on-going growth of interest even more important. Though seasoned collectors and quilt makers have "read it all before" in the many books written on the subject, a new generation has not. This book is an attempt to help their interest grow by simplifying quilt collecting. After all, in the beginning there was nothing complicated about the concept of quilts and quilt making, despite the present-day attempts to give it snob-appeal. Consider that now people are making careers out of buying, selling, writing, and lecturing about quilts, as well as conserving them. As in other areas of antiques' collecting, there is a lot of fancy talk. These days quilts are "conserved," not restored or repaired. Then, there is the matter of cleaning a quilt. I can't help but wonder what my grandmother would think about all of the "expert" advice on ways to store and preserve her handiwork, that several generations had washed with homemade and (lye) soap, and then hung to dry on clotheslines. More's the miracle, they are still in pretty good shape. At least mine are. Don't misunderstand me. I'm all for using the latest methods to care for fragile quilts. They need all the help they can get.

CHAPTER 1

How the Great Quilt Quest Began

Before you can become an "Instant Expert" on quilts or any other collectible, you should know what brought about the current interest in the subject. This gives you a perspective on what to expect, which is very important for a beginning collector. While it would be nice to be "first" in a collecting category, not all of us had that foresight, or were around at the start of a new collecting trend. In the case of quilts, while the market has developed, there are still attics waiting to yield old quilts. There are still ample opportunities to build affordable collections. Knowing the past gives you an edge on present collecting.

There are many terms and words that are an official part of the quilter's vocabulary. If you aren't familiar with them, the glossary in the back of the book will answer your questions.

The first official recognition of quilts as an art form can probably be traced to the eve of the Bicentennial. Before that, in 1971 to be exact, the Whitney Museum of American Art displayed them along with time-honored paintings and artists; not as folk art or needlework but important and historical American

Blazing Star. *Pieced and appliquéd calico quilt made in Ohio. Brightly colored patches arranged in a Star of Bethlehem pattern with borders of trailing vines. Shell quilting. Late nineteenth/early twentieth century. 96 in. × 90 in.*

(Courtesy of Sotheby's) ©1996 by Sotheby's.

art. Decorators quickly picked up on the idea, using them as decorative accessories such as wall hangings. Magazines began depicting room settings using quilts in various ways. Collectors, introduced to the dramatic possibilities of color and design found in many of the old quilts, began combing shops and attics. By 1976, quilt collecting had become big time. Quilts joined other examples of American antiques that are now acceptable as collectible. Beginning in that Bicentennial year, a growing number of "quilters" made them a project. Serious research on quilt history began around the country and many papers were published.

One of the first things quilt collectors learned was, that like old pattern glass, quilt patterns had a variety of names. Among the most common were Texas Star and Tumbling Blocks. Often, just as with pattern glass, the names had little to do with the visual design. Quilts weren't just colorful curiosities, they now had names. In order to properly catalog and evaluate them, collectors had to get acquainted with both the names and the many variations of patterns that would come under a single, basic name.

Collectors were eager for more information, and a myriad of books were published to accommodate them. Collectors knew quilts had "arrived" when they began appearing in Price Guides. Suddenly a quilt was not just a "quilt" or an object with sentimental value, it was something of monetary value.

Immediately, collectors began wondering why one quilt had a price tag of over a thousand dollars and another cost only fifteen dollars? Knowing what to look for became as important as the hunt. How old did a quilt have to be to be collected? What about patterns that seemed to have endless variations, like the large star patterns?

During the last two decades as more information has become available, collectors have become more selective. As you are about to learn, age isn't the only criteria for buying or selling quilts.

OLD QUILTS COME TO MARKET

During and after the 1976 Bicentennial, old quilts began showing up at the early Sotheby's Americana auctions. Prices were for the most part several hundred dollars per quilt. The important thing was that they were coming for auction at all. Patterns were being identified, dated, and pictured on the auction catalogue pages. Prices realized gave would-be collectors an idea of values.

Over a decade later, Sotheby's Americana Auction, held on January 30, 1988, offered a major quilt collection that was to raise the prices of quilts as well as collector interest. The Mary Strickler's Quilt collection, from the gallery of the same name just outside San Francisco, had opened in 1972. It was named after one of the prize quilts, a Mariner's Compass with trapunto feathered wreaths signed and dated "Mary R. Strickler, 1834." The shop was named "Mary Strickler's Quilt." Owners Julie Silber and Linda Ann Reuther's inventory of fine and rare quilts grew. For the first time the marketplace

Mariner's Compass. *Pieced and appliquéd quilt made in the nineteenth century. Blue, yellow, green, red, pink printed calico patches. Borders with scrolling and blossoming vines. Some discoloration with patches on reverse. 99 in. × 83 in.*

(*Courtesy of Sotheby's*) ©1996 by Sotheby's.

presented quilts as cultural documents, "examining the lives of ordinary, uncelebrated American women and reconnecting them to the lives of the people who made, used, and lived with them," stated Linda Ann Reuther in the Sotheby's catalogue. When they sold their gallery in 1988, putting their merchandise on the auction block, it was a landmark event for the quilt market.

At that auction, a rare and important Album quilt, c. 1848 sold for a whopping $110,000. It was one of fifty known Baltimore Album quilts, attributed to Mary Evans. She did many quilts for commission in the 1840s and 50s (twelve are known to exist). Another Album quilt c. 1850-1870, not as fine, sold for only $4,400. However, a unique Civil War quilt sold at Sotheby's in 1991 for a record $267,000. But, as Sotheby's expert Nancy Druckman notes, "we haven't seen anything of this quality since. If we did, the price would be even higher."

Now, collectors had a frame of reference for pricing as well as for different types to seek out. Amish quilts, for example, were represented at auction and they fetched from $2,500 to $5,575. They had yet to become trendy...and more costly.

Proof of growing quilt importance are the major corporations who have been forming collections for the last several years. They offer the public an opportunity to get acquainted with the many looks of quilt art, before beginning collections of their own. These exhibitions have recently begun traveling. Check your local museums for upcoming quilt art shows.

Currently it is usually in major cities like New York, Chicago, and Houston, where art galleries represent quilt artists and hold exhibits. However, there is scarcely a town or city that doesn't have quilt shops and quilting groups where old and new examples are displayed, sold, and created. This is true of not only the United States but countries around the world.

QUILT CONCEPTS

Yesterday
The ancestor of today's quilts was padded clothing and coverlets, first discovered by the Crusaders in the Middle East. They brought the quilted material, worn beneath their armor, on their return to the British Isles. However, it took the Great Freeze of the fourteenth century for quilting to come into general use not only for warm clothing, but for bedcovers. Shortly, the quilt was a household necessity throughout Europe, with each country developing its own type of stitchery and designs. English quilts are heavier than American since their purpose was mainly warmth.

To the nineteenth century housewife, her scrap bag was as important as the soup pot. The end result, the quilt, had to warm a bed, and add a touch of color. However, there was another purpose.

Primitive Garden. *Pieced and appliquéd quilt probably made in New Jersey in the nineteenth century. 94 1/2 in. × 89 in.*
(Courtesy of Sotheby's) ©1996 by Sotheby's.

Memories were sewn into the designs. Bits and pieces of fabric from family members and friends that related to special, cherished events, such as weddings and christenings, were used, as were work clothes and a favorite dress. Often, they became a family custom and as such, an important part of American lifestyles in the nineteenth century that is being carried over. They were given and exchanged to commemorate an important family event, like an anniversary. The Album quilt is the perfect example of a quilt made specifically for giving.

Many quilts were only put out when company came, or on special occasions. These "best" quilts show little wear and when found, they are usually in mint condition.

Quilting as a Social Event

From the late-eighteenth to almost mid-nineteenth century, women would spend evenings, often together, cutting cloth scraps into pieces to later be arranged in interesting designs. These working get-togethers became known as "quilting bees." When the women had to travel long distances, they began early in the day, often in shifts.

The quilting bee often turned into a quilting party where the women socialized as they worked together on a single quilt. At the end of the project, families joined the quilters for food and fun, and to admire the finished handiwork. Often quilt parties turned into community events, with entire families getting together.

The development of and travel to new frontiers brought about a change in the quilting bee. By the 1840s the quilting bee became a strictly female event. The pioneer woman usually did the piecing at home. She got together with other quilters to use what was often the only quilting frame in the area.

Quilts and quilt making briefly went out of fashion after the Civil War. It was the Centennial of 1876 that revived interest in Colonial furnishings and, along with it, quilts and quilting. However, it was short-lived. By the end of the nineteenth century once again quilts were sent to the attic.

The Great Depression of the 1930s made thrift a necessity. Fabric scraps were once again "bagged" to later be pieced in new patterns. Those lucky enough to have sewing machines, used them. Other Depression-era quilts were completely hand sewn.

The next great "creative" quilt spurt was the late 1950s, following World War II. It was the "do-it-yourself" era, and that included quilts. However, it was a different type of quilt. Quilters were encouraged to create their own designs and do everything by hand. But, as stated earlier, it wasn't till the Bicentennial of 1976 that quilt making in traditional forms was revived.

$\mathcal{D}$EVELOP AN EXPERT EYE BEFORE YOU BUY

Quilting began with a frame...a simple, home-made object resembling a curtain stretcher. Its purpose was to hold the patchwork tightly so that the decorative top quilt, the inner lining (stuffing) of cotton or wool, and the backing could be sewn together. The quilt was "rolled" from each of the four sides until the center was reached and the quilt finished. Generally there were two quilting frames and as many as twelve women working on the quilts. It wasn't unusual for several quilts to be finished in an all-day session.

Quilt tops were often made by one designer, but the actual quilting was done by others.

Sometimes Italian quilting was used but strictly for decoration, not for warmth. Double rows of quilting stitchery were sewn thru two layers of cloth and a narrow channel was made thru which cord or roving was introduced from the back. The lower layer of material had to be somewhat coarsely woven to allow for the introduction of the cord and for additional padding with wool or cotton.

The invention of the sewing machine in the 1840s meant that by the end of the 1860s most of the quilts were pieced by machine. However, needlework was still a "ladies" pastime. Therefore, it was only the concept of quilt making as a hobby, rather than as a necessity, that changed. *The quality of the work became of major importance.*

THE FINE ART OF STITCHING

CLUE. *To check for skillful needlework, look on the all-white counterpanes on the underside. There, in the absence of color and bright designs, only the delicate finesse of expert needlecraft stands out. The more and tinier the stitches, the finer the quilt. For instance, in a fine quilt twelve to fourteen stitches per inch would be top quality. Some old Amish quilts have been found with twenty stitches per inch.*

CLUE. *In the late nineteenth century machine stitching was used mostly on the borders. However, Crazy quilt pieces had to be pieced by hand because of the use of various fabrics, such as silks. Otherwise they buckled. If such a quilt shows machine stitching, chances are it is not of the period.*

HOW THE PIECES WERE PUT TOGETHER

Pieced and Patchwork

First made in the latter part of the eighteenth century are those in which the patterns follow geometric designs, like mosaics laboriously contrived of hundreds of small squares and diamonds. At first these small pieces were sewn directly onto a fabric backing.

By 1800 women had developed a more practical method and made the quilt parts in block units, each a portion of the overall design scheme. These blocks were pieced together in rows or diagonal bands, with strips of latticework or alternate white blocks between them. When plain white blocks were used as alternate separations they were also elaborately quilted.

The patchwork counterpanes of the nineteenth

Mosaic. Also known as the Honeycomb, it is a pieced silk grosgrain made at the turn-of-the-century. Composed of over 33,000 gold, bronze, and blue pieces, it is backed with a maroon silk with a flounced edge. 74 in. × 88 in.
(Courtesy of Sotheby's) ©1996 by Sotheby's.

century were usually made of solid colored or printed cotton fabrics, alternating with white for contrast. A favorite color scheme combined turkey red with green cotton, appliquéd on white.

Quilted stitching on the white background, perhaps in a lozenge diaper pattern or in squared criss-crossing pattern, added textural interest to the plain areas. No matter how elaborate the patchwork designs, the stitching of the quilted portions greatly enhanced the attractiveness of the spread. This was the gauge by which quilts were judged in contests.

It was quilting, rather than piecing, that required the highest degree of needlework. Some women

BLOCK PATCH TERMS. Designs are also known by their number of patches. For instance, a one patch design is a pattern made up of a single piece cut from a fabric. The number of squares on the side of a quilt block relate to which patch number category it is. For instance, a five-patch block will have five pieces on the side. Combinations and sizes of block varied over the years.

were superior in cutting and sewing the patches, but could never quite master the quilting techniques.

APPLIQUÉD QUILTING

An appliqué quilt was considered the true test of a quilt maker's talent. It was a separate, complete design stitched on top of the block. The technique differed somewhat from that of patchwork, though often the two methods were combined on a single spread. While patchwork produced a mosaic textile, appliqué was constructed from individual pieces which were sewn onto a background fabric. The central part of the design sometimes contained a large, single unit like Tree Of Life. More often a smaller unit was repeated in diaper fashions four, nine, or sixteen times to cover the quilt area. Chintz or other printed cotton was cut up to form the decorative elements and added lively interest to the plain fabrics.

At first designs were based on early painted cotton wall-hangings and bedspreads. Most fabrics

Whigs Defeat, variation. Appliquéd with red, yellow, and green swags. Made in the late nineteenth century. 80 in. × 80 in.

Collection of Anne Gilbert.

Cherry Tree. Appliqué & embroidery made c. 1930s with the embroidery done in 1960.

(Courtesy of Amy Goodhart collection)

were imported from England.

By 1850 appliquéd patchwork had become so elaborate that it was too precious for everyday use. Often the quilts became showpieces, ceasing to serve as coverlets.

Sometimes it took years to complete an intricate pattern. A close scrutiny of the more complicated appliquéd quilts will show a basket of Tulips and Little Red Schoolhouse, when repeated forty or fifty times for the quilt's central area, took up most of the work. The completion of such a quilt could have easily taken hundreds of hours.

Embroidered

Popular from 1915 thru the 1940s were cross-stitched, embroidered designs. They were often mass produced as "kit patterns." Among the patterns were Strawberries, House and around 1915 Storybook, with characters from children's tales, often in turkey red. Even though quilt "kits" and printed paper patterns for quilts were first introduced to American quilters toward the end of the nineteenth century, it wasn't until the 1920s that they became popular. Purists have commented that quilts made from a kit are on the same level as

Strawberries. *A kit quilt, embroidered, and made
in the early twentieth century.*
(Collection of Anne Gilbert)

"paint-by-number-art." This is due to their lack of individuality. After all, such kits included everything needed to make a quilt. One company, Paragon, has made kits from the 1930s thru today.

Fancy Stitches

Decorative stitching typified the Victorian "overdo" attitude. Whether for lap top quilts or Crazy quilts, stitching in contrasting colors and motifs of everything from scallops to crosses was used. The chain stitch, herringbone stitch, and all kinds of fagotting were popular. Many different types of stitches were used on the same quilt.

RECOGNIZING TYPES

Not only are there many patterns but many classifications of quilts. Within these categories are an equally large number of patterns and designs. Each type has a name. Some are related to a certain region such as Pennsylvania and Indiana Amish, and Baltimore, Maryland Album quilts.

African American & Slave

There is much controversy about this category, or even if it should be listed as a "type." Author/African-American quilt expert Cuesta Ben-

African American. *Pieced and embroidered with yellow and green square each with a bird, fowl, butterfly, or animal. Embroidered detailing. Provenance: Elsie Burns, East St. Louis, Missouri.*

(Collection of Amy Goodhart)

berry says: "I have not seen any quilts having an African influence, during my forty years of research." She went on to say that "in the case of 'slave' produced quilts, their talents depended on the skills of their mistress, who instructed them." Benberry also pointed out that when descendants of former slaves moved to Liberia and Sierra Leone, they took their quilt making skills with them. Their work resembles nineteenth century American quilts, such as the use of large block designs.

CLUES. *According to African-American quilt expert, Dr. Maude Southwell Wahlman, there are seven clues to help identify African-American quilts. They are:* vertical strips *that relate to a West African tradition of Strip Quilts,* bold, bright colors, overly large designs, multiple-patterning, asymmetry, symbolic forms, *and in the twentieth century, especially with contemporary quilters,* improvisation. *It is a field that still requires much research and study.*

Baltimore Album quilt. *Center block with eagle and flag c. 1846–56.*

(*Courtesy of Sotheby's*) ©1996 by Sotheby's.

Album

Album quilts, made in Baltimore, Maryland, between 1846 and 1854 are considered the finest examples of American quilting. The name "album" was taken from the popular pastime in the early nineteenth century of putting mementos into scrapbooks. The Album quilts carried out this concept with cloth squares. Each square had a central motif, such as a flowering tree or animal. They were made by a single designer, a combination of people working together, or several makers, each using their own creative motifs.

Many of the appliqué squares show such diverse subjects as identifiable Baltimore buildings, a soldier on horseback, or an overall geometric pattern. Religious motifs were also used. Their intricate piecing and appliqués have never been equaled.

Album bridal quilts were (and are) something special. Stitches were often so fine they are nearly imperceptible. Sometimes small details were penned with India ink, not embroidered, on an appliqué. Each square was supposedly made by a different friend of the bride and autographed by the maker.

Many Album quilt tops have survived unquilted.

Amish

When you think Amish quilts, think bold colors and large geometric patterns. The Amish, whose teachings stated "be in, but not of the world," rarely use printed fabrics. Quilt designs and colors varied from region to region. For instance, Ohio quilters pieced together multicolored rectangles in repeated patterns like Roman Stripe. In Lancaster County, Pennsylvania, the central design was a large square and the borders were wide. They are pieced and appliquéd. Other early patterns were Center Diamond, Sunshine and Shadow, Bars, Nine Patch, Baskets, and Broken Star.

Amish, Sunshine and Shadows. *Pieced wool with pink, beige, red, and black patches and a wide purple border, heightened with meandering floral vine quilting. Made in the twentieth century. 80 in. × 73 in.*

(Courtesy of Sotheby's) ©1996 by Sotheby's.

Though the Amish religion forbade the use of printed materials, they could still use bright, true colors. Perhaps the most striking things about their colors was their use of black as a color. The effect is dramatic and once you stand before an Amish quilt you'll never forget it. Expect unusual uses of color such as red with purple.

Today, there are more than 100,000 Amish in America, living in twenty states. The majority of the Amish quilts that we are familiar with come from communities clustered in Indiana, Ohio, and Pennsylvania.

Crazy Quilts

They were so-named because they had no fixed design. The early Crazy quilts, dating to Colonial times, were strictly utilitarian, created for warmth, as were covers for bed, windows, and doors. Scraps at hand were fitted together like a picture puzzle.

Before 1750, bedding and beds were considered important and awarded in wills. As cloth became more abundant, pieced quilts became more elaborate, and the Crazy quilt was discarded or forgotten. Not until the 1870s was the Crazy quilt

Crazy quilt.
Made in the turn-of-the-century of mixed fabrics and showing wear.
(Collection of Anne Gilbert)

revived. Because the fabrics were different, the quilt had its own look. It began to show up in the parlor as a "slumber robe" or a couch throw. At that time it was overall sheet size, 90 to 108 inches. Though the quilts were still made of scraps, the bits and pieces were of silk, velvet, brocade, plush, satin, wool, cotton, and linen. It was made up of large blocks of small patches, each large block fitting in a given area an equal number of times. It first became known as the "crazy patch quilt." Each block was hand-sewn to a backing of coarsely woven material. When in place, they were connected with fancy stitchery in variously colored threads.

Sometimes the blocks were embroidered like a picture, delicately embroidered with flowers, bugs, and spiders. There were also outlined birds, animals, flowers, people, and names. Other devices used were hand paintings or India ink drawings on silk or satin, advertisements or pictures printed on satin, and woven silk badges, especially those with historical significance. Sometimes the design in the material itself was accentuated with an outline stitch. The more elaborate, the more interesting the quilt, and, the more valuable.

Crib
Crib quilts, made in every pattern and classification, are not tied to any particular region. Currently, they are one of the most popular and they are sometimes expensive. One reason is fewer small quilts were made and even fewer have survived. For example, only one miniature of a Baltimore Album quilt is known to exist. It is the bold, colorful Amish crib quilts from Lancaster County, Pennsylvania, that collectors are paying top dollar for these days.

Freedom Quilts
When American patriotic fervor rose in times of war or to celebrate some historic event, quilt makers made their contribution with the so-called Patriotic or Freedom quilts. Depending on the year, they were based on such symbols as the Stars

Pinwheel.
A pieced crib quilt
with double-sided
sawtooth border and
a red background.
Made c. nineteenth
century.
(Courtesy of Amy Goodhart collection)

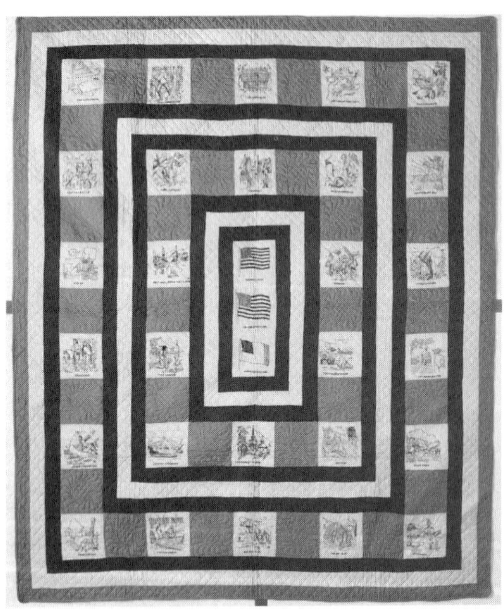

Historical. Pieced and embroidered quilt signed Alice
Mahoney, Salmon, Idaho and dated 1931. Red, white, and
blue fabric centered with Colonies' flag, the United States'
flag, and the Confederate flag, surrounded by twenty-eight
embroidered historical vignettes, and inscribed on the verso.
Diamond and flowerhead quilted background. 90 in. × 76 in.
(Courtesy of Sotheby's) ©1996 by Sotheby's.

and Stripes, the American bald eagle, and American heroes and statesmen. The American eagle was the most used symbol for quilters in the early nineteenth century. The War of 1812, the Civil War, and the Spanish-American War revived these symbols. When America celebrated the 1876 Centennial and the 1976 Bicentennial, the eagle was a dominant theme.

Friendship

Friendship quilts are considered a spin-off of the album quilts, popular in the 1840s. Their name comes from the groups of "friends" working together on the quilt. They used block patterns with each block made by a different person and then assembled and quilted by the group. Before it was pieced together, each person embroidered their signature or name on their block.

Hawaiian (Kapa)

Developed from the missionaries' patchwork, these quilts were fashioned of two whole pieces of material and appliquéd in a free-style Island motif, usually in one color on white. The quilting, done freehand, "follows the pattern." Pattern designs might be naturalistic, associated with some place or historical theme, among them baskets of flowers, ferns, turtles, and the crescent moon. But the most popular pattern was the Breadfruit. The originator of a design named it, and often a design was dedicated to a person as a mark of respect.

Log Cabin

Easy to identify, a part of their design always looks like the logs that were stacked in pioneer homes. They are symbolic of the actual log cabins. The center square is usually red, depicting the placement of the hearth or fireplace.

Log Cabin, Streaks of Lightening.
A pieced quilt with red and blues, etc. diamonds on white background. Opposite side is log cabin. Made in the turn-of-the-century.
(Courtesy of Amy Goodhart collection)

Sampling

American women sometimes made a "sampling" of patchwork or applied patterns and combined them in one quilt.

Signature

A popular custom, used to raise money for a variety of causes, was to fill a quilt with embroidered signatures. While their heyday was around the last half of the nineteenth century, they are still being made today. In the past, for a small amount of money, your name was embroidered on the quilt. When it was filled, the quilt was raffled off or given away.

Mennonite

Like the Amish, the Mennonites made quilts that have distinct religious and regional characteristics. Humility was considered an important virtue and solid colors were used to express it. However, they were lavish with their quilting. Both the Mennonites and the Amish favored stripes or simple bar designs. The Mennonites referred to the patterns with biblical connotations like "Rainbow or Joseph's Coat."

> **SHOW QUILTS.** This is a category that overlaps and includes other classifications. For example, a Log Cagin quilt may also be a Show Quilt, as can a Crazy quilt. The one thing that makes them Show Quilts is that they were made strictly for display purposes, not utilitarian.
>
> Silk was the usual material for show quilts made from the late eighteenth thru the nineteenth century. The Show Quilt became a fashion statement, when silk was no longer too rare or expensive by mid-nineteenth century. Popular patterns such as the "Star of Bethlehem" were adapted from their original cotton usage.

Theorem or Thematic

You don't hear too much about these quilts or see them at quilt shows, probably because the most unusual examples are extremely rare. They fall into two distinct categories: Advertising silks and Theorem embroidered to teach sewing techniques or simply to educate (usually children).

ADVERTISING SILKS. Made from "cigarette" silks, these were the silk patches made from specially printed advertising giveaways popular around the turn of the century. They were very colorful and the subjects varied from Indians to baseball players to the flags of the world. Quilt collectors have to compete with advertising collectors for these quilts.

THEOREM. Designs for the Theorem quilts made in the nineteenth century depended on the creativity of the maker. Those made in the twentieth century were usually made from kits.

Transfer Iron-Ons.

In the early twentieth century, designs and figures could be ironed onto a quilted surface. They were then outlined with red embroidery.

> **TRAPUNTO WORK.** Popular in the early nineteenth century, but was out of vogue after the Civil War...a help in dating a Trapunto quilt.

Trapunto

This form of quilting was used in fourteenth-century Italy. It was used from around 1800 thru the Civil War. Two layers of cloth were stitched together with a design; popular examples were flowers and vines. The use of batting stuffing in the largest design areas gives it a raised look.

CLUE. *The earliest examples were white on white. Later, Trapunto tops were apt to be put together on a sewing machine, but hand finished.*

Whole Cloth

This is a simplistic style quilt, and is made, just as the name describes, from a single piece of fabric. These could be a colored calico print, or an all white "bride's" quilt. These are known as "whitework." Amish quilts often use this technique with a solid color top. Whole cloth quilts rely on fine quilting for their appeal.

CENTRAL MEDALLION MOTIFS

While this type of quilt was popular in eighteenth - century Europe, it was in use in America in the early nineteenth century. Two of the most often produced Central Medallion quilt motifs were florals and the "Tree of Life." The designs were appliquéd. From the 1850s to 90s, the designs were in solid colors and calicos. They had a variety of pattern names including Mariner's Compass and Princess Feather. By the 1920s, new floral patterns were used along with prevailing pastel colors. From the 1920s to 40s they were finished with scalloped borders.

Geometric. A patchwork quilt made c. 1860s in Indiana. Blue and white in color, it has cotton seeds and worn areas. 75 in. × 80 in. (Collection of Anne Gilbert)

Geometric Designs

The use of geometric designs came into use somewhere in the 1840s. This quilt consisted of pieced triangle, rectangle, and square shapes that were sometimes combined. There were even patches of minute, postage stamp size.

WHAT YOU SHOULD KNOW ABOUT PATTERNS

How They Were Used

The patterns for quilting were indicated on the material by pencil, chalk, or charcoal, depending on the color of the fabric. Since it was easier to seam two straight edges, the geometric pattern evolved along straight lines, running laterally, diagonally, or coming radially from a central point. Thousands of designs resulted and each had its own fanciful name.

What's in a Name?

Often a single pattern was given different names in widely separated regions, but it was not uncommon to find the same name applied to several unrelated designs. For instance, Bear's Paw in Ohio, or Duck

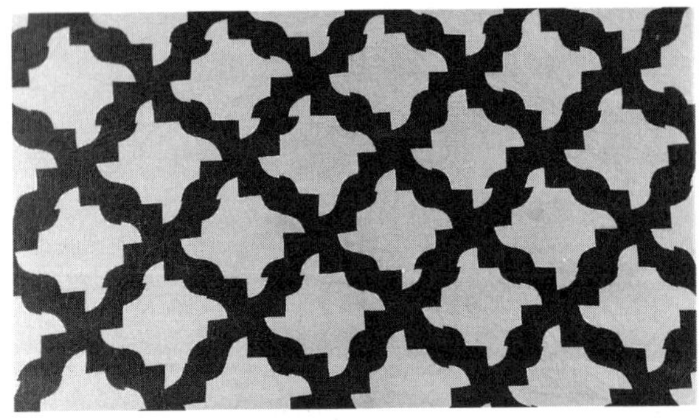

Drunkard's Path. *A pieced red and white quilt made c. 1890–1900. 80 in. × 80 in.*
(Collection of Amy Goodhart)

Feet in the Mud in New York. It became Hand of Friendship in Pennsylvania.

There are star patterns named for every state in the Union, derived from the basic Star of Bethlehem, an eight-point star found in numerous interpretations. Entire volumes have been devoted to describing these quilts with quaint and charming names such as Flying Geese, Drunkard's Path, and Hearts and Gizzards.

HOW SOME QUILTS GOT HISTORICAL NAMES

The Pine Tree

This pattern, created during the Revolutionary War period, is one of the oldest. It was used in all thirteen original states and was in honor of the Colonist's Pine Tree Flag.

The Union Quilt

After 1782 appliqué eagle quilts became popular. But, when used in the north, briefly, during the Civil War, the pattern was named Union.

The Road to California

During the western migration of the 1860s, this pattern depicted stylized motifs of wagon wheels and chains.

The Little Giant

Named in honor of Stephen A. Douglas, when he debated Abraham Lincoln.

The Slave Chain

Originally this pattern without intervening blocks was named "Job's Tears." It was known as the Slave Chain during the years when Missouri sought statehood, and whether it was to be a "slave" or "free" state was the issue of the day. It went thru another name change in the 1840s, when it became Texas Tears, and Texas was trying to join the Union.

Patterns as Symbols

Many of the patterns used in early quilts first came about as symbols, among them the health sign (reverse of bent cross), baskets, and pine trees. The empty basket was viewed as a symbol of female charitable giving. One of the most important was the pine tree, symbolizing home and shelter. In different sections of the country the meanings varied, as did the names, e.g., Tree of Life and Tree Everlasting.

Birds were often used as symbols. Stylized peacock feathers in patchwork and lovebirds on a Baltimore Bride's quilt are examples commonly found.

Variation of Indian Trails. *Patchwork blue and white quilt made in the late nineteenth century.*

(Courtesy of a private collector)

Basket. *Blue and pink pastels with an inscribed signature,
"Made by grandma Harwood."*
(Collection of Amy Goodhart)

Some Popular Patterns

BASKET. The Basket pattern began as an appliquéd basket-with-urn motif in nineteenth-century Medallion quilts. The familiar pieced, triangular form, came about after 1860. It can be found in single or mixed colors, in bold as well as pastels.

BIRD IN AIR. There are many variations of one of the earliest patchwork patterns. Basically, pieced patches were cut out in triangular shapes, all the same size. The patches forming the pattern may be two-color or whatever was in the scrap bag.

Basket, variation. *Summer quilt.*
(Collection of Amy Goodhart)

Double wedding ring. *Pieced and appliquéd quilt with pastel pinks, blues, and yellows made c. 1920s.*

(Collection of Anne Gilbert)

DOUBLE WEDDING RING. This is among the most popular patterns, with symbolic interlocking wedding rings. While it was first known to have existed around 1876, it was used most often in the 1930s. Legend has it that its origins began with the interlocking wedding ring, "gimmel," used by Pennsylvania German immigrants.

DRESDEN PLATE. This pattern first appeared in the 1840s. Because of its circular motif it was one of the easier patterns for beginners. By the 1930s it used synthetic dyes and often combined pastels with bright prints.

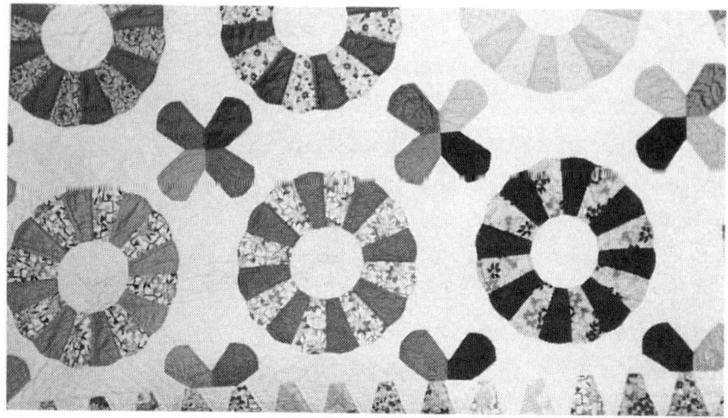

Dresden Plate, variation. *Pieced and appliquéd quilt with pastels, pinks, and blues made c. 1920s.*

(Collection of Amy Goodhart)

Dresden Plate, variation. Pieced and patchwork quilt with
bright reds, greens, and yellows made c. 1920s. 80 in. × 80 in.
(Collection of Anne Gilbert)

DRUNKARD'S PATH. This pattern is an example of
how politics and social issues influenced quilting.
Originally Drunkard's Path was called, "Robbing
Peter To Pay Paul." In 1874, when the Women's
Christian Temperance Union was founded, women
used quilts as banners. The colors were often blue
and white, the WCTU colors. During that time the
name was changed to Pumpkin Vine. There are
many variations of the pattern, but it always uses
curved patches. Other names include Rocky Road
to Kansas, Solomon's Puzzle, and World's Puzzle.

GRANDMOTHER'S FLOWER GARDEN. Though
there are many variations of this popular pattern,
the most traditional is geometric shapes pieced in
circles. The pattern came into use in the late nineteenth century, with floral centers in a plain color.
In the Depression years of the 1920s and 30s, the
look changed with the use of whatever scraps (usually printed) were at hand.

TIP. *The Instant Expert will judge patterns like
Grandmother's Flower Garden and Dresden Plate by
how good the overall colors appear. Not every quilt
maker had an "eye for color." How the colors blend
affects the value of the quilt.*
  *When the pattern changes from a circular shape to a
diamond, its name changes to reflect the pattern change,*

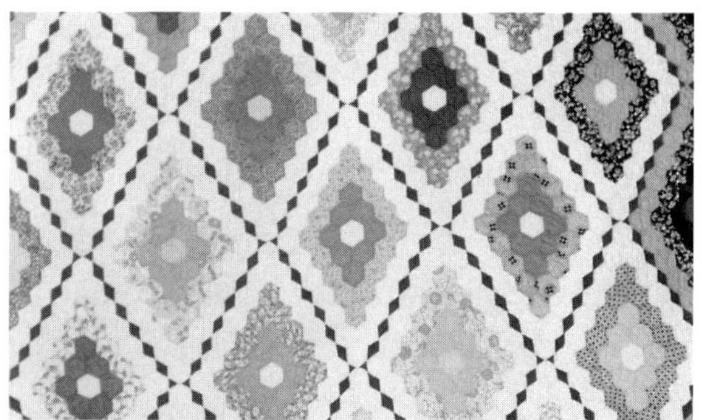

Field of Diamonds, variation. *Pieced and appliquéd hexagons assembled in a diamond shape, made c. 1930s.*

(Collection of Amy Goodhart)

e.g., Diamond Field, Rainbow Tiles, or Field of Diamonds. Flower Garden theme quilts have been made since the early eighteenth century. At that time the hexagons were pieced together using templates and an overcast stitch. The fabric was pressed around a paper template. The paper was removed after the pieces were sewn together. If a quilt still has some paper templates, and shows the use of the overcast stitch, it may be an early rarity.

IRISH CHAIN. In single, double, triple, this pattern dates to the 1840s and continues to fascinate quilters and collectors. It can be changed from its basic nine patch block pattern using one color and a

Geometric, Double Irish chain stitch. *Blue and white calico quilt on white. Made in the nineteenth century. 80 in. × 80 in.*

(Collection of Anne Gilbert)

Feathered Stars. _Patchwork quilt made c. 1880._
(Collection of Sandy Mason)

Lonestar or Texas. _Patchwork and pieced multi-colored
quilt made c. 1910. 74 in. × 80 in._
(Courtesy of Kavanagh's Antiques)

**_Eight-Pointed
Star._**
_Pieced multi-
colored quilt made
c. 1850–60.
98 in. × 98 in._
_(Collection of
Amy Goodhart)_

white block, to any number of patches and several color combinations. Because of its "optical illusion" effect, it goes well in contemporary homes.

SCHOOL HOUSE. The most usual form resembles a traditional schoolhouse, but there are many variations. It is as simple as a child's drawing as it repeats in rows.

STARS. Stars and variations have been patterns since early American days. Probably the earliest of these is the eight-point star, dating back to the mid-eighteenth century.

LONE STAR. This and other star patterns have never stopped being made by quilt makers. The large, central star is cut and pieced. The surrounding myriad of free-cut stars required great precision in cutting. The use of the super-size central star didn't come into use until the late nineteenth and early twentieth centuries.

STAR OF BETHLEHEM. Examples are known to

Star of Bethlehem. Composed of brightly colored red, yellow, russet, green, and slate blue calico and chintz patches arranged in a Star of Bethlehem pattern. At center a red and yellow paisley chintz pinwheel. Some restoration and net conservation, made in southeastern Pennsylvania in 1830–50. 116 in. × 116 in.

(Courtesy of Sotheby's) ©1996 by Sotheby's.

exist dating from the 1830s. When well executed, quilts with this pattern can be among the most expensive pieced. The central star is large, and surrounded by hundreds of identically-sized diamonds, sewn from the center.

> **RARE STAR OF BETHLEHEM QUILT.** The Star of Bethlehem is composed of identically-sized diamonds, sewn from a center, each ever-widening row a different color from the preceding row. The piecing requires great accuracy, as the slightest mistake in the inner sections becomes increasingly magnified in succeeding rows. Excerpted from Homage to Amanda.

MOSAIC. Just as its name implies, thousands of tiny patches were arranged in a pattern reminiscent of millifiore glass, or magnified natural crystals. The end result is almost dimensional to the eye.

WHIGS DEFEAT. This pattern was developed in 1856, when the last presidential candidate of the Whig party, General Winfield Scott, was defeated. The Whig party was created to oppose the democratic party of Andrew Jackson.

NOTE: Additional pattern names are listed under References at the back of the book.

*Two **Whig Rose** variations.* *Whig Rose Pennsylvania shows a variety of techniques. Another variation of Whig Rose, pieced and appliqué quilt with a pastel blue background with deep red roses, stylized. Made in the twentieth century.*

(Both from the Collection of Amy Goodhart)

WHEN A QUILT HAS A "FLAW"

The Instant Expert will know that what looks like a mistake in a quilt can actually be *purposely done*. The "flaw" could be a star or flower left out of one block. This practice dates back to the nineteenth century, especially in regions like Pennsylvania where religion was a major influence. The saying, handed down to explain these omissions, is: "Only God makes something perfect." The "flaw" can be in a piece of patchwork that differs in color from

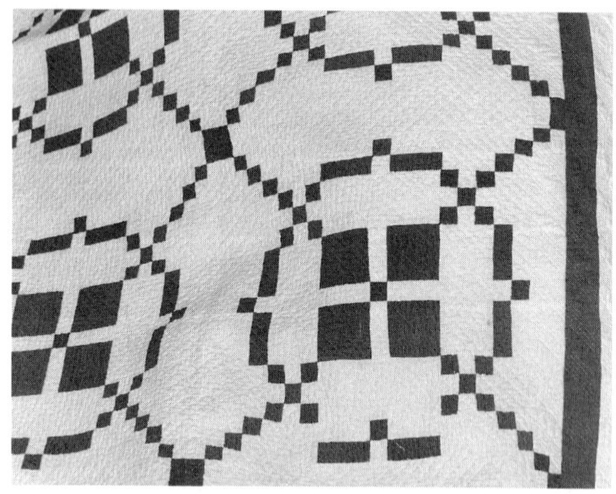

Burgoyne Surrounded. *Pieced red and white quilt made c. 1850–60. It has "Nobody's perfect but God" imperfect block.* (Collection of Amy Goodhart)

the rest of the pattern, or in the stitching pattern. Some collectors feel this makes a quilt more interesting, and even more valuable.

TIP. *Hidden messages can sometimes be found on quilts. Look on the white-on-white stitching pattern. Since they are practically invisible it will take a lot of looking. This was popular in the early twentieth century. An example would be, "I love you."*

The Dating Game: How to Date Quilts Like an Expert

> **SUNBONNET SUE.** One of the most popular patterns, originated in the early 1900s. Not until the 1920s did quilt makers around the country make it fashionable. It has never stopped being made.

Is it as old as it looks? There are many ways to date a quilt even when it isn't signed or dated. Examining colors, patterns, fabrics, techniques, and styles of the quilts are a few ways.

CLUE. *Be forewarned! A quilt may have some of the above features, but still not be as old as it looks. A quilt showing work not in keeping with its historical period is permissible only if it has been professionally conserved.*

DATING BY COLORS

Colors available to early quilt makers depended on what plants were available to harmonize with the fabric fibers they had on hand. One of their major problems was finding plants and fiber combinations that would be colorfast.

The colors included turkey red, indigo, and browns made from the roots of the madder plant. Black was made from logwood and yellow from a tree in the West Indies. The only native commercial dye crop was Indigo, and that was grown mostly in the Carolinas.

Dyes were homemade until the 1860s. Dye recipes were handed down in families and printed in *Godey's Lady's Book*. It was common to dye entire bolts of cloth at one time. This "piece" dying is still done in some parts of the country today, but usually with commercial dyes.

By the middle of the nineteenth century the creation of aniline dyes brought colorfast greens, alizarin red, mauves, and new shades of brown.

BLACK. This color can date quilts by examining the fabric dyed with it. For instance, from 1890 to 1925 it was used in cotton quilts. Earlier, in 1860 thru the early twentieth century, it was used with silk. From 1890 to the first quarter of the twentieth century, black was used in wool quilts.

BLUE. In many shades, blue has been in use for hundreds of years. For early American quilt makers, Indigo was the only proven, colorfast dyestuff at hand until the mid-nineteenth century. Since it was still in use in the 1880s, it isn't a reliable way to date a quilt, unless all other factors are in agreement. Since aniline dyes replaced early dyestuff in the 1850s, new shades of blue were introduced. A light blue with a hint of violet would date a quilt from the 1870s–1890s. A grayish blue was used as a background color for prints in the 1890s.

BROWNS. Browns have been made in a variety of tones since early times. What was at hand in nature determined the shade. For instance, in the South where red dirt was available, clay-pot brown was made. Cloth was buried in the soil and the end

Single Princess Feather. Indigo blue and white quilt made c. 1880. Provenance: Carrie Williams May, Amsterdam, New York. 72 in. × 86 in.

(Collection of Amy Goodhart)

result was terra-cotta. For deep browns, black walnut and butternut shells were used as dyes. From the late eighteenth century to around 1856, dyes were made by individuals and manufacturers. These used vegetable, animal, or mineral sources.

GRAY. This color was used after the 1940s when it became a fashionable color for clothing.

GREENS. Greens weren't successfully dyed until the late eighteenth century. By 1875 greens were used, but over the years they faded to tan, mustard, or khaki. If foliage has these tinges it could have been made from 1875 to 1900. If your quilt "greens" appear to be dark green, this would date it to the late nineteenth century. What is called "Nile green" was made during the 1920s and 30s.

PASTELS. In the 1920s thru the 40s, further improvements in colorfast dyes resulted in not only purples but lavender, orchid, raspberry, and lilac.

In the 1920s thru late 1940s peach, melon, and tangerine shades were used.

PURPLE. This color first became popular during the Civil War era. Various shades were used, taking advantage of the new synthetic dyes.

Patchwork. *Made in the late nineteenth century.*
(Collection of Anne Gilbert)

Appliqué and embroidery quilt with a raised floral motif, bars, and nine patch cornerstone in pastels, made in the 1930s. 84 in. x 84 in.
(Courtesy of Sandy Mason)

REDS. One of the earliest dyestuffs to make red was Madder. The color it made is known as turkey red. Learning its color tones helps separate it from other reds. Turkey red dates thru the nineteenth century to the 1830s and 40s. If faded, it would date the quilt to between 1875 and 1925.

CLUE. *When true turkey red ages it retains its bright color. When synthetic dyes were used the color faded to either brown or pink, and eventually to white.*

Texas Star. *Patchwork quilt in tan, teal, and brown. The combination of tan, teal, and brown places it in the early twentieth century.*

(*Courtesy of Marge's Antiques*)

RUST TONES. Used from 1885 to around 1910.

TANS. Quilts dyed predominantly with tans date from the 1860s thru the 1880s. This is a result of inferior synthetic dyes. Originally greens, over the years they faded to tan.

CLUES. *Tans and browns are difficult to date because they faded over the years due to laundering and age. Another problem is that greens, even red, blue, and purple, faded over the years to different shades of brown. Therefore, if the brown is vibrant, the quilt probably dates to the twentieth century.*

YELLOW. This was an early quilt color, even dating to the Colonies in the 1660s. It was a bland shade. If the yellow in your quilt has an orange-yellow hue, butterscotch, true orange, burnt orange, or is a calico with a yellow background, it would date to the late nineteenth century.

Color Combinations

Quilt colors that used white with one single color were popular in the 1840s. Most common were green and turkey red. When two color quilts became fashionable, the colors used with white were green and red, and navy and red. Combinations of blacks, blues, and grays probably date to the early twentieth century.

DATING BY PRINTED FABRICS

Printed fabrics offer another clue to age. One of the first printed fabrics used in America—Chintz—came from England in the eighteenth century. However, by 1720 American printers and engravers began making printed calico, linen, and silk from copper plate designs.

By the 1830s there were many textile mills producing more than floral prints. Historical, patriotic, and agricultural scenes were favorite motifs printed on Chintz and calico (calicoe).

> **PRINTED COTTON SWATCHES AND SWATCHBOOKS.** Add knowledge and interest to collections. Periodically, they turn up at auctions of textiles.

Chintz

Originally Chintz was brought to England from India by sixteenth century traders. The Hindu word "chitta" translates to "spotted cloth." Chintz patterns over the years have continued to use the India-influenced designs. It imitated the look of silk by glazing the cotton.

American Chintz quilts from the eighteenth to mid-nineteenth century were either appliquéd cut-out or pieced scrap in design.

> **OLD FABRICS.** Can be found in unlikely places. Go thru the "rag bag" at thrift stores, estate, and garage sales.

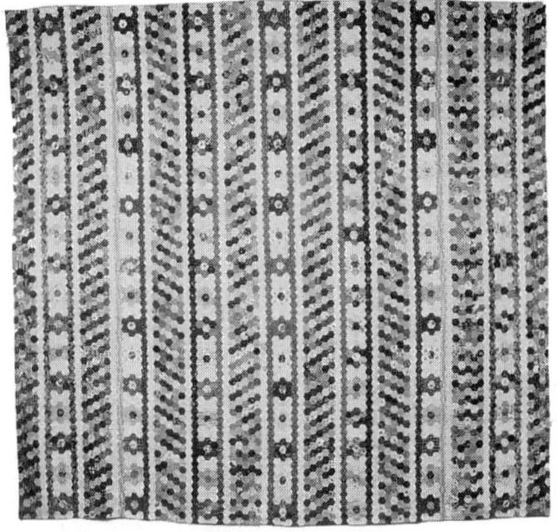

Pieced Calico quilt top. *American quilt made in the nineteenth century. Pinwheels and bars on red, blue, green, beige, and cream, mounted on white cotton backing.*
$87\,^1/_2$ in. $\times$ $87\,^1/_2$ in.

(Courtesy of Skinner Gallery)

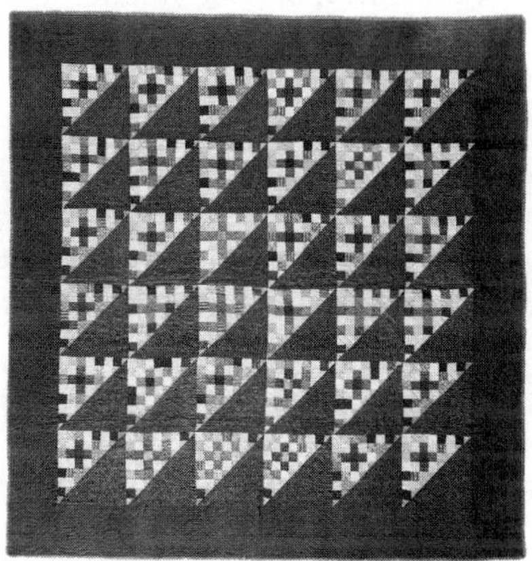

Bird in Flight. *Pieced calico quilt in pink, blue, and green with printed patches within a wide green calico border and heightened with rope quilting. 76 in. x 76 in.*

(Courtesy of Sotheby's) ©1996 by Sotheby's.

Calico

This cotton fabric used small, figured designs. It can be dated by referring to the aforementioned colors, when combined with a print motif.

Homespun

Most homespun is from linen and wool. While it was commonplace when American women spun their own cloth, it was practically obsolete by the late 1830s. Homespun can sometimes be recognized by thread irregularities and loose weaving. Unfortunately, this isn't a foolproof method. Homespun-type fabric continues to be made. Check for other age characteristics such as color.

Sarsenet Cambric

This was a silky textured cotton used from the beginning of the nineteenth century to around 1875.

Cretonne

Large prints characterized this unglazed twill weave. Originally its use was for upholstery and drapery. Eventually, it became another scrap material for the quilt maker. It was made from 1880 to the 1920s.

Satin

During the 1920s the Yo-yo quilt and other "puff" styles became popular. The fashion lasted until around 1950s.

TIP. *Puff style quilts were mass produced by the 1950s.*

PROBLEMS

Is it Really Patchwork?

At first glance it may look like patchwork, but a closer look may prove it is actually Cheater's Cloth. It was made in the 1850s. The patterns that resembled patchwork were actually an illusion of chintz prints. In the early twentieth century they copied Log Cabin motifs. By 1933 Cheater's Cloth was being marketed by Sears Roebuck in Dresden Plate, Double Wedding Ring, and Grandmother's Flower Garden. For quilt fanciers who were too busy to "do it from scratch," it was the easy way.

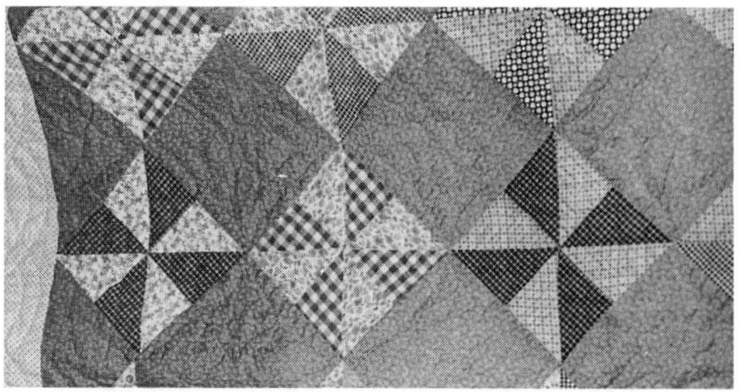

Windmill pattern. Not as old as it looks, this quilt is patchwork with cable stitched-quilted border and homespun backing. Made in Pennsylvania, patches date from the 1890s to 1930s, mixing old colors with pastels. 72 in. × 82 in.

(Courtesy of Kavanagh's Antiques)

What to Look for

After you've found a quilt you like, have someone hold it up for you and step back about ten feet to look at the pattern. The first thing to look for are the obvious spots, rips, and faded places. Then, look for water marks, fold creases, medicine stains, and disintegration. Next, move in close and check for any fabric replacement. Workmanship is important. In a pieced quilt, points should not be cut off and pieces should match evenly. The edges of appliquéd quilts should be smoothly turned under, and the stitches should be either decorative or blind. The sewing should be done with neat, tiny stitching. It would be nice to say every dealer is an expert, when they tell you a quilt is all original and old. Unfortunately, they may not actually know. It's up to you to know.

Copies

Reproductions of old quilt patterns are nothing new. The time-honored "School House" and "Bear Paws," like many others have been made over and over since they were first introduced. However, just as in other areas of collecting, if a quilt was made during the period when the pattern was first introduced, it would be considered a period piece, and

Flying geese. *This is one of the many old patterns being reproduced. However, this is an authentic old pieced quilt in red and white, made c. 1900s.*

(Collection of Sandy Mason)

its price would reflect its age. The problem began during the 1976 Bicentennial celebration when there was a revival of interest in quilting. The Smithsonian sold rights to reproduce early American quilt patterns to China. From then on it was open season on reproductions.

As Amy Goodhart, collector of quilts, told me: "The perfect example of what happened in quilting reproductions is the School House pattern. It was reproduced in India and showed up at antique shows several years ago as 'old American' priced at $2,600. Later collectors found it at shows for $900. It now turns up in a variety of mail-order catalogues for around $150. The blue and white 'Bear Claw' pattern also turns up in catalogues." She also pointed out that these and other reproductions all but killed the collector's quilt market. Finally, thanks to quilt study groups and educated collectors (Instant Experts) the market is making a comeback and prices are rising.

Expect to find the most traditional patterns reproduced, among them Baskets, Double Wedding Ring, and various geometric block patterns.

Some have four to six stitches per inch, though they are advertised as handquilted. They are sold in crib, full, queen, and king sizes (they didn't have king-sized beds until the twentieth century, though beds were sometimes made to accommodate several children).

Laura Fisher advises to watch for reproductions that are factory made in China, Haiti, and India. Amish-looking quilts are coming out of China. After the copyright dates are removed they are run thru auctions as old. "The Chinese copies have big stitches and the figures are 'cookie cutter'—too perfect, not like hand cut." She also noted that because crib quilts are popular and hard to come by, "unscrupulous dealers have cut old, large quilts into crib size, rebound them and sold as crib quilts." Another popular rarity are black stereotype figures, Uncle Sam, and flag motifs. Generally they are pieced and on tea-dyed muslin ecru. The size is 30" x 36" and they can sell for $1,400. However, you can find them on the back of many country catalogs for far less. She also advises if you like the look of Amish quilts, to buy new and pay "new" prices, rather than pay antique prices for a new reproduction. "Read and look. Adjust your eye."

Some quilt motifs, such as baskets, have been used in overall quilt patterns since the 1840s. They have shown up in variations from the stylized Amish type with a straight-line handle to pastel designs of the 1920s. Reproductions of both are currently being made.

Replacement Rip-Offs

Just like in buying antique furniture, a quilt can be a "married piece." This means major parts have been replaced. Or possibly, an entire quilt built around a central part of the pattern.

Crib quilt fakery is going on all too frequently today. A worn, old quilt, is cut down and rebound into the small, "trendy" crib size. One way to check it out is by the pattern. If it is too big for the quilt size it is a "cut down."

LOOK ON THE BACK. Are the stitching patterns not in keeping with the front?

CHECK THE FABRIC. Can any supposedly nineteenth century quilt be made with a dacron or polyester batting? Or nylon thread?

How to Study the Marketplace:

ANALYZING THE STATE OF THE MARKET

Basically, whether it is quilts, or any other type of antique or collectible, the market is divided into several parts. Each offers the collector a potential source. The one exception is the picker, who sells only to dealers. At the picker level you too can scour the countryside. Despite what you may hear, attics, barns, and basements are never totally wiped out by professionals (pickers, etc.). Just ask yourself what happened when someone in your family moved or inherited objects? First of all, not everybody likes the same type of thing. Nor does everybody know the true value of a "quilt" or other antique. What happens is usually one of the following: (1) they hold a garage sale, (2) give the item away to the Salvation Army, (3) throw it out, (4) have an estate sale (where there are many objects), (5) call in a dealer, (6) call in an appraiser before putting it up for sale, (7) put it in a consignment shop or a church rummage

> **AUCTION ADVICE.** Always attend an auction preview. It will be your only chance to carefully study the quilts up for auction. A good opportunity to save you from getting "carried away" at bidding time, without really knowing what you are bidding on.

sale, or (8) put it up at auction. "Where" depends on how much they know about the items.

As you can see, there are plenty of opportunities, if you go looking before the picker does. It is the picker who is your basic competitor. The picker buys for a tiny fraction of the value and sells to a dealer. The dealer increases the price or, if it is a rarity, may send it to a major auction house. Depending on how knowledgeable the dealer is, the collector may buy a valuable quilt for far less than its value. It happens everyday, and it can happen anywhere.

TIP. *Remember, antiques travel far from home. You could find a rare American quilt just about anywhere in*

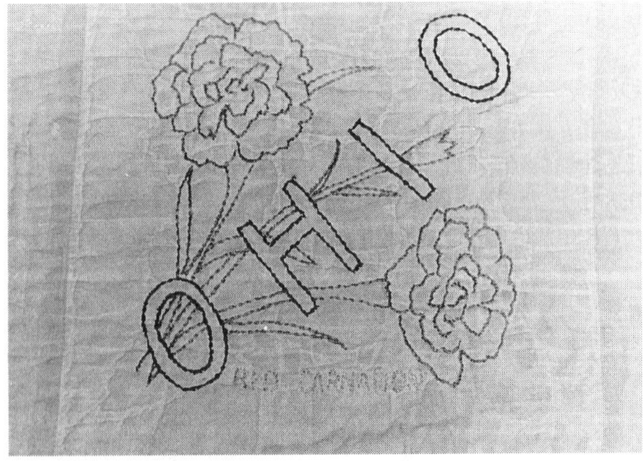

States and State Flowers. *A garage sale find for $25, this quilt has forty-eight states with embroidery in black and pinks and bordered in chartreuse. Made c. 1940s. 86 in. × 86 in.*

(Collection of Anne Gilbert)

Album Blocks. *Pieced cotton and calico quilt with red, brown, blue, and yellow. The background heightened with shell quilting made c. 1878. 74 in. × 66 in.*

(Courtesy of Sotheby's) © 1996 by Sotheby's.

the world. I remember when I was in Honolulu several years ago, I did what I always do on a trip, went to a yard sale. Among other things I found a fine, Victorian Crazy quilt for $10, and in good condition. Chatting with the seller, I learned she had lived in Boston and moved to Hawaii in the 1970s. She had taken family antiques with her. While she hadn't particularly liked the quilt, she'd stuffed it into a box to protect a ceramic lamp.

What's happening in the quilt marketplace depends on who you talk to. Think of it as just like getting opinions from three doctors before you have an operation. In the end you have to make up

CORPORATIONS COLLECT QUILTS. Bank of America in Boca Raton has a magnificent "Show Quilt" displayed in their offices. Johnson and Johnson and Citibank have contemporary quilts on their walls. Art Quilts are in the collections of Arthur Anderson, Chicago, Illinois and Hyperion, Glendale, California.

your own mind. So it is with buying quilts. Opinions differ. As you are about to learn, markets differ in regions.

Museum Shows

If you want to know what's about to be trendy in collecting, keep track of museum shows in major cities. It doesn't matter whether it's the introductory exhibit of the Arts and Crafts movement, or American quilts. This is usually followed by a traveling exhibit and publication of a book on the subject. After this, there are usually major auctions in the category, held around the country. The end result is a revived interest and raising of prices in the category.

Over the years the Museum of American Folk Art has held exhibits from its quilt collection. Most recently (May 4–September 8, 1996) the Museum held a major quilt exhibit and published a book on the exhibit. What is (and was) important from a collector's standpoint, is that it showed all the major American quilt making traditions from early examples to the contemporary quilt winners of the Great American Quilt Festival contests. It also offered a wonderful opportunity for collectors to get the overall scope of American quilt making. And, to get a close-up of the myriad of types.

ADVICE FROM EXPERTS

"The quilt market has been soft since 1991," according to Sotheby's folk art expert, Nancy Druckman. "People (collectors) are satiated...and running out of space." Druckman, who recalls the 1991 world record for an American Quilt ($267,000) says: "It would take something really terrific to shake up the market. There are too many repros available, and run-of-the-mill types." She also observed that people who buy quilts for everyday use (and display on beds) are buying the reproductions. "They are more durable than old quilts. You can get the effect of 'old' while using them."

Laura Fisher, a New York dealer who can be called the Doyenné of the quilts, was one of the first to include quilts as part of Americana decor. When she speaks, collectors listen.

"Crazy quilts are highly sought after. They were considered 'best' or 'company quilts' even when made. Look around. Find the best quality and condition. Unless it is so unusual, give yourself time to look around. Just because it is old doesn't make it good."

Speaking from a dealer's point of view, she has found that "once more antique quilts are on the upsurge. There was a little dip for awhile. Now they are so much a part of our lives that we see them in product ads and on magazine covers. They are even in our word usage, e.g., 'crazy quilt of laws.'"

Amy Goodhart is a collector from Miami, Florida. Her interest began in the 1980s. "I had been involved in crafts. When there was the '76 revival, I was fascinated. It was a natural progression to move to quilt collecting. I have fifty old quilts. A few are real treasures, such as a star quilt I purchased for $75. A 1910 embroidery quilt was found for $100 in a New Hampshire junk shop.

Geometrics. *Pieced quilt in blue and white with blue saw-tooth border, this quilt's inscription adds provenance—and desirability. It is signed and inscribed: "Grandma Thompson made this quilt when she was 81 years old for her great grandchild, Burnic Power." Made c. 1898*

(Collection of Amy Goodhart, one of her "treasures")

"My grandmother's quilts from Paducah, Kentucky, are an inherited treasure. Most I display stacked in an open cupboard. Also, over the back of benches and on an old apple ladder. I have hung a Twelve Crowns as art. I neither quilt nor appraise." Goodhart is active in the Florida "Search For Quilts" group.

Manya Sheehan, Expert-Leslie Hindman Auctioneers, Chicago, Illinois says: "We have sold a variety of quilts over the years. Currently the market is strong. The quilts with historical significance, such as the spread wing American eagle or House pattern, do well. Amish quilts are of great interest. Those we handle most are from Indiana, Ohio, and New York. The Mrs. Flowers collection-sale in April of 1993 had some important examples. One Amish quilt sold for $14,000. As always the earliest sold best.

"The value of later quilts depends on the intricacy of the design, the quality of the materials...and condition."

Anne Petrone, the Americana Specialist at Skin-

House and birds.
Embroidered quilt with greens, pinks, and blues, and a meandering floral border made c. 1930s. 66 in. × 92 in.
(Courtesy of Kavanagh's Antiques)

ner Auctions in Boston/Bolton, Massachusetts says: "The market is not what it was in the late 80s. We do best with nineteenth century appliqués. The highest bid recently was for a nineteenth century appliqué that brought $4,000. Amish quilts are doing well. Crazy quilts, unless they have unusual pieces such as tobacco ribbons, sell for $300 to $500."

She also mentioned that while collectors display the nineteenth century quilts, the twentieth century ones are used. She also feels that twentieth century quilts are undervalued and are a good buy for beginning collectors.

Dealer Linda Reuther's shop in California, Hearts and Hands Galleries, has been selling quilts around the San Francisco Bay area, in San Anselmo, since 1972. "The fakes that have come to market have changed the whole quilt collecting concept," she said. "While people buy them to use on beds, the authentic quilts are for hanging and decorating." She pointed out, that as a result, "collectors look for quilts with visuals and graphics." Among her best sellers are those with a geometric pattern that is used as a graphic, such as Log Cabin quilts.

PRICES

> DEALERS MAY BE YOUR BEST SOURCE...IF: (1) you aren't as knowledgeable as they are about fabrics, workmanship, etc., and (2) you have more money than time.

Prices can vary from region to region. This can be the result of the popularity of patterns and the lifestyles in different areas. Heavier type quilts, like Crazy quilts, are usually more sought after in cold climates than in places like Florida.

Old quilts at fairs usually range from $200 to $2,500. A new quilt will start out at $600 and go up.

A utility quilt from the 30s or 40s can cost from $250 to $500 in good condition and with a simple design. Museum quality old quilts have sold for $100,000 and more at auction.

Some Price Ranges - Dealer

Double Wedding Ring 1930	$250–$700
Tumbling Block	$850–$1,200
Snowflakes	$600–$800
Amish crib quilt	$650–$3,500
Traditional crib quilt	$375–$750
Lonestar	$750–$975
Crazy quilts	$400–$800
Embroidered kit cross stitch	$250–$450
Embroidered kit cross stitch inscribed, or with some individual work	$900–$1,200
American tufted Candlewick coverlet (dated 1822)	$1,200
Egyptian Revival coverlet (Scarab design)	$400

Auction Prices

PATCHWORK

American Patchwork quilt, 19th Century, in the Tulip pattern, in yellow, green, and red calico. *88 × 86 inches.* **$300**

American Patchwork quilt, in the Diamond pattern, in green and gold. *100 × 76 inches.* **$450**

American Patchwork quilt, 19th Century, in the Star pattern, with a feather border, in blue, red, and green calico. *88 × 68 inches.* **$450**

American Patchwork quilt, mid-19th Century, in the Trailing Rose pattern, in shades of red and green. *84 × 88 inches.* **$800**

American Patchwork quilt, third quarter 19th Century, in the Oak Leaf pattern, in shades of brown, red, and gold. *84 × 82 inches.* **$450**

American Patchwork quilt, mid-19th Century, in the Star and Block pattern in rose and brown surrounded by a floral chintz border. *96 × 94 inches.* **$225**

American Patchwork Double Irish Chain quilt, 19th Century, comprised of tan lattice work motif. *72 × 70 inches.* **$200**

Friendly Cow. *Appliquéd cotton and wool quilt in red, brown, green, ocher, and beige patches with a cow, apple tree, blossoms, and a fence. Made c. 1928. This is a good example of what it takes for 20s and 30s quilts to come to market big time. 76 1/2 in. × 64 in.*

(Courtesy of Sotheby's) ©1996 by Sotheby's.

American Patchwork quilt, 19th Century, in the Wild Goose Chase pattern, in blue and white. *64 × 60 inches.*
$425

American Patchwork quilt, in the Chain Block pattern, in green, yellow, and red. *98 × 78 inches.* **$800**

American Patchwork quilt, 19th Century, in the Desert Rose pattern, in shades of red, gold, and green, signed *Mrs. C. Ogden* and dated *1845. 90 × 92 inches.* **$2,700**

American Patchwork quilt, 19th Century, in the Block and Star pattern, in red, blue, and brown calico. *82 × 90 inches.*
$350

American Patchwork quilt, mid-19th Century, in the Block and Leaf pattern, in shades of green, gold, and red. *68 × 66 inches.* **$325**

American Patchwork quilt, third quarter 19th Century, having rose and tulip design, in peach, green, and gold. *82 × 72 inches.* **$550**

American Patchwork quilt, mid-19th Century, in the Sunburst pattern, in red, blue, yellow, and green calico on a pink field with chintz floral borders. *100 × 96 inches.*   **$800**

American Patchwork quilt, in the Triangular and Diamond pattern, in rose calico. *76 × 62 inches.*   **$80**

American Patchwork quilt, with floral blossom and leaf design surrounded by scalloped border, in red and green. *100 × 80 inches.*   **$160**

American Patchwork quilt, 19th Century, in the Compass Rose pattern, in shades of red and light green. *82 × 82 inches.*   **$350**

Pair of American Patchwork quilts, in the Band of Daisies pattern, in green and yellow with scalloped border. Each: *84 × 72 inches.*   **$225**

Pair of American Patchwork quilts, in the Diagonal Block pattern, in peach. *74 × 74 inches.*   **$425**

American Patchwork quilt, early 19th Century, having Star Medallion surrounded by four spread winged eagles, holding branches in their mouths, and stars. *78 × 70 inches.*   **$1,900**

American Patchwork quilt, late 19th century, in the House Pattern, in red, green, and blue calico on yellow ground. *76 × 72 inches.*   **$500**

American Patchwork quilt, 19th Century, in the Tulip and Trailing Vine pattern, in red and green calico. *70 × 80 inches.*   **$225**

American Patchwork quilt, late 19th Century, in the Star of David pattern, in red, blue, yellow, green, and other. *82 × 82 inches.*   **$450**

American Patchwork quilt, in the Star and Block pattern, in red, green, and brown. *80 × 64 inches.*   **$250**

American Patchwork quilt, in the Block pattern, in shades of brown, rose, and cream calico. *76 × 90 inches.*   **$180**

American Patchwork quilt, 19th Century, with decorated cornucopia issuing flowers surrounded by a foliate and floral border, in shades of blue, rose, red, and green. *100 × 80 inches.*   **$1,000**

American Patchwork quilt, in the Morning Glory pattern, in shades of light blue, lavender, pink, and rose. *90 × 74 inches.*   **$325**

American Patchwork quilt, mid-19th Century, in the Princess Feather pattern in shades of red and green calico. *90 × 90 inches.*   **$550**

American Patchwork quilt, mid-19th Century, in the Sunrise pattern, in red calico. *100 × 100 inches.* **$190**

American Patchwork quilt, having a floral bouquet surrounded by a floral border, in light pink, green, purple, and yellow. *90 × 66 inches.* **$475**

American Patchwork Prairie Star quilt, circa 1920, Missouri, the Star comprised of dark shading to light yellow diamonds, on yellow ground. *78 ¹/₂ × 76 inches.* **$350**

American calico Patchwork Spider Web quilt, circa 1940, comprised of pieced octagonals against a sky blue ground. *90 × 72 inches.* **$275**

American calico Patchwork Courthouse Square quilt, comprised of blue, red, and rose blocks. *76 × 74 inches.* **$110**

American calico Patchwork Star quilt, Third Quarter, 19th Century, comprised of four pink stars. *79 × 75 inches.* **$100**

American Patchwork calico quilt, late 19th Century, in the Star of David pattern, in polychrome calico. *35 × 88 inches.* **$700**

American calico Patchwork quilt, comprised of stars within light green borders. *85 × 72 inches.* **$170**

American calico Patchwork Bear Paw quilt, early 20th Century, comprised of red bear claws divided by zigzag calico bands on a white ground. *82 × 72 inches.* **$325**

American calico Patchwork King David's Crown quilt, circa 1930, comprised of polychrome calico elongated squares against a yellow ground. *86 × 74 inches.* **$300**

American calico Patchwork School House quilt, late 19th century, New York, comprised of four bands of red and blue school houses. *65 × 84 inches.* **$700**

American calico Patchwork Swallow quilt, late 19th Century, Indiana, with red and black calico sawtooth blocks against a white ground. *72 × 70 inches.* **$200**

American calico Delectable Mountain quilt, third quarter 19th Century, comprised of red calico sawtooth triangles against a white ground. *95 × 90 inches.* **$700**

American calico Patchwork Cathedral Window quilt, in rose, blue, yellow, and red. *72 x 69 inches.* **$110**

American calico Patchwork Kansas Troubles quilt, late 19th Century, comprised of grey, blue, and black sawtooth triangles. *82 × 74 inches.* **$450**

American Patchwork chintz quilt, second quarter 19th Century, in the Geese in Flight pattern, divided by floral bands. *92 × 92 inches.* **$375**

American Patchwork chintz quilt, mid-19th Century, with alternating diamonds of floral and geometric designs. *106 × 94 inches.* **$325**

American chintz quilt, mid-19th century, with overall floral motif. *104 × 100 inches.* **$390**

American chintz Patchwork quilt, second quarter 19th Century, in the Block and Diamond pattern, with alternating chintz and calico prints. *108 × 100 inches.* **$300**

American wool Patchwork quilt, circa 1930, comprised of rose, red, turquoise, and brown star-filled blocks. *76 × 86 inches.* **$450**

American wool Patchwork Courthouse Steps quilt, early 20th Century, comprised of purple, red, black, and tamestrips. *81 × 73 inches.* **$225**

American wool Patchwork Pineapple quilt, early 20th Century, comprised of brown, blue, and red strips. *74 × 71 inches.* **$325**

AMISH

Amish Patchwork Winged Square quilt, circa 1930, Ohio, comprised of lavender, yellow, and brown triangles on royal blue ground, framed by yellow border. *78 × 68 inches.* **$200**

Amish Patchwork Pinwheel quilt, Ohio, comprised of six bands of pink, green, yellow, and blue pinwheels against a teal ground. *88 × 78 inches.* **$1,000**

Amish pieced quilt, circa 1910, having repeating tricolor medallions pieced from hexagonal patches, in rust, navy, blue, and beige. *65 × 74 inches.* **$130**

Amish pieced quilt, circa 1910, lattice design each square containing four nine-patch squares. *67 × 53 inches.* **$750**

Amish wool Sawtooth Diamond in Square quilt, circa 1900, Lancaster County, with green diamond and square on crimson ground. *76 × 76 inches.* **$3,400**

Amish cotton Blazing Star quilt, circa 1920, Ohio, with four bands of lavender and yellow stars against a green ground framed by lavender border. *75 × 66 inches.* **$750**

Amish cotton and chintz Basket quilt, circa 1920, Ohio, comprised of purple, magenta, and mint green baskets and green ground, framed with magenta border. *82 × 80 inches.* **$1,300**

Amish cotton Basket quilt, dated Tuesday, February 11th, 1924, with maroon and blue baskets against a purple ground framed by maroon border. *85 × 72 inches.*   **$3,000**

Amish polished cotton Star in Square Crib quilt, 20th Century, Ohio, with a slate blue, rust, and rose star within a maroon frame on blue ground. *46 × 43 inches.*   **$250**

Amish sateen and cotton Double Wedding Ring quilt, circa1930, Ohio, worked in pink, red, lavender, purple, yellow, and green against a black ground.   **$5,000**

Amish cotton sateen Bar quilt, circa 1910, Ohio, with royal blue bars against a black ground with black border. *85 × 65 inches.*   **$2,800**

Amish cotton sateen Abstract Tree quilt, circa 1910, Ohio, comprised of lavender, blue, brown, and red diamonds against a black ground framed by chestnut border. *85 × 72 inches.*   **$5,000**

Amish polished cotton Ocean Wave quilt, circa 1910, Ohio, with multi-banded trellis worked in triangles of blue, green, and lavender on a black ground framed by cornflower blue border. *73 × 73 inches.*   **$2,000**

Amish cotton sateen Lightning Streak quilt, circa 1920, comprised of black, purple, olive green, and maroon diagonal bands with a royal blue frame and black border. *80 × 73 inches.*   **$2,000**

Amish wool Triple Irish Chain quilt, late 19th Century. Lancaster County, having red and green trellis on slate blue ground with green corner squares, initialed M.S.   **$3,000**

Amish wool Bar quilt, circa 1920, Lancaster County, comprised of crimson and turquoise bars framed by rose bars and olive green border, with embroidered initials on reverse. *85 × 76 inches.*   **$3,400**

MENNONITE

Mennonite Patchwork Double Irish Chain quilt, early 20th Century, Pennsylvania, having red and yellow trellis on green ground with red sawtooth border. *86 1/2 × 86 1/2 inches.*   **$850**

Mennonite cotton and calico Feathered Star quilt, third quarter 19th century, Pennsylvania, comprised of chestnut feathered stars within a yellow calico border against a green ground. *72 × 72 inches.*   **$800**

CRAZY QUILT

American Victorian Crazy quilt, third quarter 19th Century, in velvet and silk block motif, embroidered with floral sprays, fans, stars, and other surrounding an American flag. *74 × 61 inches.*   **$1,500**

American Crazy quilt, circa 1920, with irregular shaped pieced cloth with embroidered floral designs. *69 × 75 inches.*   **$110**

American Victorian velvet Crazy quilt, late 19th Century, comprised of velvet patches surrounded by embroidery. *86 × 70 inches.*   **$750**

Victorian silk and velvet Album Crazy quilt, late 19th Century, comprised of polychrome pieces embroidered with flowers, fan, spider web, and other. *64 × 64 inches.*
$1,100

LOG CABIN

American wool Patchwork Log Cabin quilt, circa 1900, comprised of purple, pink, tan, and grey diamonds on a black ground, not backed. *77 × 68 inches.*   **$350**

Pair of American Patchwork quilts, in the Log Cabin pattern, with alternating light and dark diagonal bands. Each: *78 × 62 inches.*   **$1,200**

American calico Patchwork Log Cabin quilt, comprised of blue, red, and tan strips. *80 × 72 inches.*   **$350**

American calico Patchwork Log Cabin quilt, comprised of red, blue, gold, and black pierced diamonds, surrounded by black calico border. *60 × 70 inches.*   **$450**

American Patchwork Log Cabin quilt, late 19th Century, in pink and white. *83 × 71 inches.*   **$200**

American calico Patchwork Reversible Log Cabin and Light and Dark Crosses quilt, comprised of calico pieced squares, the reverse with calico crosses. *79 × 66 inches.* **$450**

CRIB

American Patchwork Crib quilt, third quarter 19th Century, having a rose medallion surrounded by foliage and a grape and vine border, together with a Log Cabin patterned quilt. Former: *80 × 42 inches.*   **$850**

American Appliqué Crib quilt, circa 1950, appliquéd with a cowboy and Indians, embroidered "Ride 'em Cowboy." *69 × 47 inches.*   **$250**

American calico Patchwork Crib quilt, early 20th Century, comprised of polychrome calico triangles. *76 × 53 inches.*   **$160**

DOLL

American Patchwork Tree Everlasting Doll quilt, late 19th Century, comprised of three sawtooth bars on white ground. *37 × 37 inches.* **$325**

GLAZES WORSTED

American indigo glazed Worsted quilt, circa 1800, quilted diamond blocks of alternating floral motifs and parallel lines. *102 × 96 inches.* **$1,200**

APPLIQUÊ

American Appliqué Rose quilt, Third Quarter 19th century, comprised of red and green roses within diamonds. *72 × 72 inches.* **$200**

American Appliqué Wig Rose quilt, Third Quarter 19th Century, comprised of red and green rose, surrounded by a rose and vine border. *86 × 82 inches.* **$500**

American Appliqué Album quilt, circa 1900, having white ground and scrolling border centering alternating floral images. *80 × 67 inches.* **$250**

Pieced silk, velvet, and satin Crazy quilt, American, late 19th Century, composed of brightly colored silk, velvet, and satin patches with embroidered, printed, and painted decoration, including figures, flowers, birds, animals, and trains within a wide royal-blue velvet border. Some staining. Approximately *68 × 68 inches.* **$977**

Pieced and Appliquéd cotton Floral Album quilt top, American, circa 1850, composed of twenty-five squares each with green, red, yellow, blue, and pink solid and calico patches with summer flower motifs. Some discoloration. Approximately *85 × 85 inches.* **$690**

Pieced cotton Irish Chain quilt, American, circa 1890, composed of slate blue, red, and white cotton patches, the field heightened with cube and diagonal line quilting. Some fading and discoloration.
Approximately 84 × 72 inches (2.13 m. x 1.83 m.) **$862**

Pieced cotton Rainbow quilt, probably Pennsylvania, circa 1859, composed of brightly colored green, blue, orange, and brown cotton patches, the field heightened with diagonal line and cable quilting.
Approximately 84 × 70 inches. **$747**

PIECED

American Pieced quilt, circa 1880, overall diamond lattice, having alternating white diamonds and red and white diamonds in a variant of the Greek Cross design, with embroidered names. *68 × 80 inches.* **$120**

American Pieced quilt, circa 1927, comprising of blocks of irregularly shaped patches of prints and solids, embroidered members of Lutheran M. Bahlman Frauenverin 1927, with a name of each member in each pieced square.
64 × 85 inches.   **$250**

American chintz quilt, mid-19th Century, with alternating floral and foliate-scrolled stripes. *90 × 88 inches.*   **$275**

American cotton Appliqué Rose Cross quilt, third quarter, 19th Century, comprised of four red, yellow, and green roses, on a rosette and diamond pattern quilted ground.
74 × 81 inches.   **$750**

While this African-American pictorial quilt didn't sell, it had an estimated auction value of $6,000–$8,000. One of the reasons was its condition. Another, though it was described as twentieth century, it did not say when, where it was made, or have any provenance.

Appliquéd cotton and wool African-American Pictorial quilt, 20th century, composed of yellow, black, purple, cream, and blue patches with two crosses, a sun, a moon, stars, a bird, six serpents, and a squirrel centering the inscription *Believe On The Lord Jesus Christ* on an army-green ground stitched in white with undulating lines. Some fading and staining. *71 $\frac{1}{2}$ × 61 $\frac{1}{2}$ inches.*

Quilting Today

CHAPTER 5

What's Happening Where

In case you don't already know, quilters are everywhere. They include women and men, with mothers teaching their children how to quilt (just like in days gone by). Regional interest continues to spawn not only groups but books, such as *Florida Quilts* by Charlotte Allen Williams. If you want to find a group in your area, you could check the Yellow Pages (that's the easy way). Another likely place is your church or temple.

For instance, some African-American women have meetings and quilting bees in their church. From Detroit to Brooklyn, the older women (according to a *New York Times* article) are part of a growing network of African-American women who consider quilting an historical and cultural art form. Virginia Hall, of Brooklyn, New York, has founded Southern African-American Quilters. They meet at the neighborhood library to learn quilting. Back in 1985, Carolyn Mazloomi of Cincinnati, Ohio, founded The Women of Color Quilter's Network. Today it has nine chapters worldwide. The oldest such group is the Daughters of Dorcas & Sons, begun sixteen years ago in Washington, D.C. by retired Army seamstress Viola V. Canady. The name has biblical connotations, coming from a New Testament seamstress.

Quilters are busy in the tropics. For instance, Patty Trevarthen, Boca Raton, Florida, founded the Gold Coast Quilter's Guild. It has 135 members. Not bad for an area that is considered tourist and seasonally transient. But, as she pointed out, "a lot of quilters and collectors are transferred from other areas."

To find a quilter's group, she suggested, "ask at quilt shops and get on the internet...What makes a quilter's group so interesting is that it transcends all age and economic barriers."

Amy Goodhart of Miami, Florida, says: "I'm a collector." Her collection of over fifty quilts not only includes some made in the 1950s, but some made before 1850. "I bought one Chicago Century of Progress quilt because of its futuristic motif,

Bridal quilt, Medallion style. *Pieced and appliquéd, this quilt was made by Eliza Woodfield Hagaman (b. 1842) between 1874 and 1897 for her daughter, with hearts, birds, leaves, diamonds, and colors, a center medallion of pieced octagons, and an inner border that is appliquéd with happy symbols. The middle border is nine patches on point with lattice.*

(Collection of Amy Goodhart)

combined with a 'World Without End' design. It was made by Aurora Dyer in Chicago in 1933 and bought directly from the Dyer family collection. It is pieced and appliquéd cotton, and a Souvenir quilt." These Chicago Century of Progress quilts were made for a contest, sponsored by Sears Roebuck. Over 35,000 quilters entered. She pointed out that these souvenir quilts are hard to find these days since so many were "even taken to the beach and picnics till they wore out."

Goodhart looks for quilts that purposely have an imperfection. One example is her "Bourgoyne Surrounded" quilt.

However, she points with pride to one quilt in particular...a Bridal quilt with quite a history. "My bridal quilt went on tour in Japan, in the 1993 Hearts To Hands quilt Festival." Goodhart related that the exhibits traveled to the quality department stores. "There are many traveling quilt exhibits these days, but this is surely one of the most unusual.

"One of the geometric designs is backwards. Quilters often did this purposely to either call attention to a section where an inscription was on the back, or with a religious connotation, that only God could create perfection."

TIP. *Goodhart advises collectors that when a "quilt strays from its pattern and color of motif, it was intentional." For instance, one of her basket quilts has one red basket. On the opposite side is an inscription. She also looks for variations of traditional designs. One example is her Double Wedding Ring quilt, with an unusual border. Another is a Whig Rose pattern that used many different quilting and sewing techniques. Like other collectors and quilters, she researches constantly and often lectures. "If you have family quilts treat them like other family treasures."*

"It is important to record provenance," advises Goodhart. "Take a piece of muslin and write everything you know about it and sew it to a corner of the quilt."

Sandy Mason, of Princeton, Wisconsin, says: "What started out as a necessity, turned into a hobby that turned into a career." Mason's first experience with quilts came when she and her husband moved from Aurora, Illinois, to Princeton, Wisconsin. Used to a home with artificial heat, they learned the best way to keep their old house warm was to cover up with quilts. "So, I would get up at 5:30, get my housework done, husband off to work, and kids off to school and then cut and sew quilt blocks till the kids came home from school. That year, 1960, I made about eighty quilt tops. At the same time I had begun exchanging quilt blocks with other quilters throughout the United States. As I was exchanging those quilt blocks, I would ask in my letters if anyone knew anything about a machine that I could use to quilt my eighty-plus quilt tops. One answer started my quilting by machine. I had become addicted to quilt making. To support my addiction I had to start selling some of my quilts so I could go out and buy more fabric for more quilts. It ended up with us owning our own quilting business. For twenty-five years I have been doing machine quilting for other people."

Today, Mason and her husband, Ronald, both do machine quilting. Their shop, Quilts and Quilting, covers every aspect of quilting from fabrics to finished products. "We have done machine quilting services all over the world, from Johannesburg, South Africa to Australia and Europe."

CONSERVATION TODAY

Conservation (restoration)

A quilt is ready for conservation if you see a broken seam, tiny tear, rip, hole, or threadbare patches. A conservator may begin with a consultation with fees starting at $35. The condition, value, and date made are studied. Cost of restoration can begin at $20 and go as high as $1,500.

Exact fabric is used whenever possible. Though

some quilts are beyond restoration, they can find new life as small wall hangings, etc.

Care

Collectors have a variety of tips for quilt care. Here are some do's and don'ts.

Dirt and oil can cause quilt fabrics to disintegrate over time. Clean by hand in the bathtub. Line the tub with a sheet, and fill it with cool water. Add the quilt and let it soak, squishing it up and down with your hands. Do this two or three times, draining the water in between, and then add a mild soap and repeat the procedure, rinsing the quilt ten times and draining the water each time.

Because the quilt is weakest when wet, grasp the four corners of the wet sheet and use it to lift the coverlet from the tub. Dry outside, face down on a dry sheet, spread on the grass.

Test before washing for colorfastness. Take a damp white washcloth and blot onto the fabric. Any exchange of color means the quilt will bleed.

Silk quilts should *not* be washed. They can be vacuumed with caution. Use a low suction vacuum cleaner and cover the quilt with a fiber glass screen to keep the fabric from being pulled and torn.

Do *not* wash in a washing machine. The agitation can tear the materials and stitches. Wash in a large sink or bathtub using the mildest detergent obtainable. Ensure or Orvus Past are preferable and available at some quilt supply shops. Never use heavy duty laundry powders or liquids. Use lukewarm water with the detergent and soak the quilt overnight. Rinse thoroughly two or three times. Handle wet quilts carefully and get help in lifting them from the water.

Taking a quilt to the cleaners is a no-no. Often the dyes are not stable in today's cleaning solvents.

DISPLAYING: Whether hanging on a wall or covering a bed, always keep quilts out of direct light. The ultra violet component of sunlight and some artificial lights can damage and fade fabrics.

A musty scent shouldn't be confused with dirt. Air the quilt. One way is to put them in the dryer on "air fluff" or lay them on a bed and turn on a paddle fan.

STORAGE: Don't store quilts in a plastic bag because plastic traps moisture. Moisture may cause climatic stains which can permanently damage quilts. It has natural fibers and must breathe. Put it in a big pillowcase or wrap it in an old sheet.

Don't store quilts in bare wooden chests, such as cedar, or on bare wooden shelves. The acid in wood can stain and damage quilts. Acid-free tissue paper, found at art supply stores or some quilt supply shops, should be used to wrap quilts. They can also be stored in large muslin covered tubes.

Don't pat the folds of the quilt, leave them loose. Refold it two or three times a year, but do not fold the same way all the time. This causes permanent creases resulting in broken threads and fibers.

WHAT TO DO WITH HEAVILY DAMAGED QUILTS

Here's proof that old quilts never die, even though they may fade away. While quilt collectors

Wearables. Patchwork wrap-around skirt made from a late nineteenth century quilt top.

(Collection of Anne Gilbert)

probably are the major purchasers of the following items, non-collectors are big buyers as well.

With little effort old quilts can become jackets, vests, skirts, dresses and blouses, purses, and hair-bows. They can also become decorative accessories like pillows, bed linens, tablecloths, window hangings, teddy bears, and other stuffed animal figures. Old quilts can even become greeting cards.

Spin-Off Collectibles

Today, most every aspect of quilting has become collectible. Sought after items may include quilt kits, paper patterns, templates, and cutouts.

Feed sack prints were used to back quilts in the 1890s when they were first produced. Even though they originally had red and blue designs and advertising, they were made to have the designs wash out. Finding a quilt that still has the original feed sack art is considered rare, a bit of history.

Feed sacks came in a variety of prints. To this day, their colors are still vivid. They were used into the early 50s for feed from the mill. And, after the sack was empty, the wife would take the bag and use it for quilt fabric. In the 1930s Depression era, fabric was hard to come by and every scrap was saved. Feed sack material was used to make clothing. Left-over pieces were used to make scrap quilts.

CLUES. *If you think you have found a feed sack, look for the perforated stitch line along the edges. It seems to never disappear. Feed sacks came in a variety of weaves. The finer the weave, the finer the contents.*

QUILT MAKING TODAY

Quilter and shop owner Sandy Mason says: "New techniques are popping up daily. Some are useful and some are just a flash in the fire. It seems for every new tool brought out there is a new book to explain how to use it. Our experience is that with the Omnigrid ruler and a rotary cutter we can do just about anything the new special (one use only)

Heaven and Earth. *An Art quilt made with cotton, cotton blends, lamé, and cotton batting. Made by Jane A. Sassaman, c. 1991. 64 in. × 64 in.*

(Courtesy of Jane A. Sassaman)

Smoke and Mirrors. *An Art quilt made by Marcia Karlin, c. 1995. The images are cyanotype and inkodye prints on cotton and silk organza. 58 ¹/₂ in. × 39 in.*

(Courtesy of Marcia Karlin)

tool can do. Today, you can buy preprinted quilt blocks (flip and sew type), preprinted squares, and triangles (freezer paper type) and if you are really looking for a fast quilt, you can buy a cheater's fabric. However, we have feed sacks printed with a cheater's Grandmother's Flower Garden pattern. Perhaps the cheaters fabrics aren't that new."

Today's Version of the Quilting Bee

Quilting is still a social as well as a work activity. While the purpose is the same the approach has added some new dimensions. These days there are revivals within quilting groups of the quilting bee and quilting party. In addition there are lectures at local civic buildings, such as the library, and at quilting shops and clubs. Conventions and exhibits, often on a worldwide scale, offer opportunities for quilters not only to exhibit or display collections of their own, but to socialize as well.

Enter the Art Quilt

The Art quilt had its roots in the Crazy quilt that also used the contemporary materials of the nineteenth century. However, what differentiates the Art quilt from its classic cousin is more than size, shape, and materials. The key element is content. These are artists' messages communicated thru the classic quilt maker's tools of color, shape, and texture. Beginning in the 1970s, fabric and fiber artists picked up on the quilting concept. The difference was that they combined new designs, materials, and techniques. Overnight, the quilter's scrap bag had become a "mixed bag." Anything and everything was "salvaged."

While traditional style quilts had pattern names, the new artists gave contemporary quilts a voice and a message. Probably the best example is the AIDS quilt where each individually-made square tells an emotional story. The quilt had a purpose other than utilitarian. It had become a medium with a message. The AIDS quilt had its beginnings on June 1987. At that time, the Names Project

Memorial Quilt was officially started. Its purpose was to commemorate individuals who had died of the AIDS virus. The quilt was made up of approximately 1,200 handmade quilt blocks, each three feet by six feet.

Since then, the Art quilt movement has spread around the world, reviving old techniques and creating contemporary examples. You may be surprised to know that there are many serious collectors of American quilts and quilt makers in Japan.

The yearly International Quilt Festival, held in Houston, Texas, attracts exhibitors worldwide. It is the largest annual quilt convention, show, sale, and quilt-making academy in the world, begun three decades ago.

TIP. *For quilters and contemporary and Art quilt collectors, the yearly commemorative International Quilt Festival Catalogue is a MUST. Not only does it tell about classes, but events, sources, and contests. Information is listed in this book under "Events."*

Where yesterday's quilt makers were unknown, except for those few who signed their work, today's quilter is known as a "quilt artist." Collectors pay big money for the growing number of recognized artists, often thousands of dollars. This has resulted in the making of miniquilts. They can decorate a small condo wall, and give collectors an opportunity to own something affordable by an important artist.

Although the vast majority of late twentieth century quilt makers are choosing the medium of layered, stuffed, and stitched fabric to create bed covers, an increasing number of artists are producing work intended to warm the spirit rather than the body.

The Art quilt has reshaped our concepts. Quilting may be viewed as an art form with a visual design that appeals to the eye. As a form of graphic art old quilts, and new, are hung on the wall. No longer is quilting a hobby or a craft, but an art form passed down from generation to generation.

Today's Art quilter combines traditional quilting techniques and twentieth century technology with artistic training to produce a personal and aesthetic statement. It is more suitable as a wall hanging than a bed covering.

While skills are important, they are a means to an end and not the sole measure of success. Rather, the primary criterion for evaluation is whether the artist has transcended technique in favor of communicating a unique idea thru fabric. By designing work for a vertical surface the quilt maker is free of the restrictions imposed by the bedcover function. With the opportunity to see the entire surface at once, the designs no longer need to be a series of repeated, related small-scale motifs that mark traditional quilts and were designed to be viewed from a close vantage point. Contemporary quilts can be any size and shape. More and more quilt artists are creating or embellishing their works with materials that might not keep out the cold and that probably should not be laundered.

The Art quilters are inspired by contemporary visual art forms including painting, video, film, photography, and computer-generated images. Many are a radical departure from traditional quilts thru the use of new diverse techniques and materials. These include ribbons, plastics, metals, silkscreen printing, lithography, Xerox transfer, Cibachrome photographs, spray prints, buttons, and glass beads.

Often the words that are part of the design may be bold and political or delicate and poetical. The Art quilts themselves are all shapes, sizes, and with stylistic approaches that range from the abstract to the pictorial.

The photographic transfer of image from film onto fabric is just one of the many new techniques.

Many quilt artists hand-dye purchased cottons and synthetic fabrics in an effort to create their own distinctive palette of colors with which to express their artistic vision. Judith H. Perry's "True Poems

Flee" shows her use of words and ranges of colors using this approach.

"Throw-away" objects such as buttons, sequins, gloves, and even plastic toys are used to embellish the surface of their quilted pictures.

Despite our increasing reliance on computer technology, the intimate and physical qualities of the handmade object have never had more appeal.

The eighteenth and nineteenth century quilt maker conceived of her quilt as a functional bed-cover which she pieced together from the fabric remnants of daily life. She and her quilt were judged by the precision of her seams and stitches and her ability to replicate traditional designs. Today's quilter combines traditional quilting techniques and twentieth century technology with artistic training to produce a personal and aesthetic statement. It is more suitable to hanging on a wall than covering a bed.

Some Important Artists and How They Work

JUDITH H. PERRY (WINNETKA, IL): "I love working with fabric (it speaks to me! Whether I have hand-dyed or commercially printed fabric, I

Jungle Nights in Harlem,
Part of a Jazz Series.
Made by Judith H. Perry, c. 1994.
Mixed media,
33 in. x 40 in.
(Courtesy of Judith H. Perry)

use the juxtaposition of pattern, color, texture, and sometimes poetry to create a very rich surface. Thru the use of this surface and the sculpted drawing line of the quilting, I create abstracted landscapes that evoke a specific quality of light and mood, while emphasizing the complicated nature of the world around and within us." Perry explores two favorite subjects, nature and jazz, with a series of quilts. "About Jazz" is her most recent series. "Quilting, like jazz, is one of our true American art forms."

JANE A. SASSAMAN (CHICAGO, IL): "Currently, I am exploring the concept of radiation. It has led me to examine the relationship between heaven and earth. So in my quilt, 'Heaven and Earth.' Heaven is a traditional idealized representation—all powerful and perfect."

Before discovering quilting she worked in many design mediums. She began to quilt in 1980. She sees her quilts as symbolic statements about the

Neon Maze. An Art quilt, silk-screened and hand-dyed fabric with some over-dyed commercial prints. Machine pieced and hand quilted by Ellen Oppenheimer. 48 in. × 50 in.
(Courtesy of the Textile Museum)

cycles and spiritual forces of life. Her quilts use colorful fabrics cut into dramatic shapes.

MARCIA KARLIN (LINCOLNSHIRE, IL): "I use the traditional medium of quilt making to subvert cultural preconceptions and explore issues of identity, marginalization, dislocation, and loss." Karlin has been working as a quilt artist for twelve years. Many of her quilt series' are based on her own life experiences. Her quilts combine the use of photographic processes (cyanotype and inkodye prints) with fabrics and found objects. They often are embroidered, appliquéd, quilted, and machine pieced.

NOTE: All of the above artists are listed in various Who's Who reference directories, books such as *Great American Quilts*, and various periodicals. They have won important awards.

Contemporary quilters have many opportunities to display and sell their works. The largest such event, the International Quilt Festival, is held yearly in Houston, Texas. Both old and contemporary quilts are offered for sale. Another is Quilt Nation at the Dairy Barn Southeastern Ohio Cultural Arts Center. It also offers an ongoing series of exhibitions. Its purpose is to promote the contemporary quilt as an art form. They hold traveling exhibitions and offer quilters many opportunities for awards.

ADDITIONAL PATTERN NAMES

NOTE: These and other patterns are pictured in pattern books for contemporary quilters to use. They can be found in quilt shops. This will give you a good frame of reference for collecting possibilities.

Bear's Track	Blazing Sun
Birds in Air	Bridal Wreath
Bird of Paradise	Bud and Rose Wreath
Blazing Star	

Cactus Flower
Caesar's Crown
California Star
Castle Wall
Cats and Mice
Children of Israel
Chintz Patch
Chips and Whetstone
Churn Dash
Circular Saw
Clay's choice
Cock's Comb
Combination Star
Compass
Conventional Tulip
Cornucopia
Country Cross Roads
Courthouse Square
Cowboy's Star
Crazy Ann
Cross and Crown
Cross Roads
Crosses and Losses
Crown and Cross
Crown and Thorns

David and Goliath
Delectable Mountains
Devil's Claws
Double Hearts
Duck Paddle
Dutch Mill
Dutchman's Puzzle

Eight Hands Round
Eight-pointed Star

Falling Timbers
Five-pointed Star
Flower Star
Flowers in a Pot
Flying Dutchman

Flying Geese
Foliage Wreath
Fool's Puzzle
Forbidden Fruit
French Star

Garden of Eden
Geometric Star
Goose Tracks
Grandmother's Choice
Grandmother's Fan
Grandmother's Favorite
Greek Cross

Hands All Around
Handy Andy
Hawaiian Grape Vine
Hearts and Flowers
Hearts and Gizzards
Hen and Chickens
Hexagon

Iowa Star
Irish Puzzle

Jack-in-the-Box
Jacob's Ladder (1)
Jacob's Ladder (2)
Jagged Edge
Job's Troubles
Joseph's Coat

Kansas Sunflower
King David's Crown
King's Crown
King's Star

Letter X
Lincoln's Platform
Little Giant
Live Oak Tree
Lobster

Lone Ring
Lone Star

Maiden Hair Fern
Maltese Cross
Melon Patch
Mexican Cross
Mexican Rose
Mexican Star
Mill Wheel
Missouri Star
Monkey Wrench
Moon Over the Mountain
Morning Star

North Carolina Lily
North Carolina Rose
North Carolina Star

Oak Leaf
Oak Leaf Wreath
Octagonal Star
Odd Fellow's Cross
Ohio Star
Old Maid's Puzzle
Old Tippecanoe

Palm Leaf
Patience Corner
Pennsylvania Dutch
Pennsylvania Dutch
   Design
Peony
Pierced Star
Pineapple
Pine Tree
Prairie Flower
Premium Star
Presentation
Puss-in-the-Corner

Queen Charlotte's Crown

Queen's Crown

Reversible Counterpane
Rising Star
Robbing Peter to Pay Paul
Rocky Road to Kansas
Rolling Pinwheel
Rolling Stone
Rose and Oak Leaf
Rose of Sharon
Rose Petal
Royal Cross
Royal Star

Saw Tooth
Secret Drawer
Silk Basket
Sister's Choice
Snail's Trail
Star and Planets
Star Flower
Star of the Four Winds
Star of the West
Star Upon Star
Stepping Stones
St. Louis Star
Storm at Sea
Sun Burst
Sun Burst Patchwork
Sunflower
Square and Cross
Sweet Gum Leaf
Swing-in-the-Center

Tea Leaf
Tennessee Star
Three Crosses
Tree of Life
Triple Sunflower
Tulip
Tulip Crib
Tulip Design

Tulip Lady Fingers
Turkey Tracks
Twinkling Star

Union Square
Union Star

Virginia's Star

Water Wheel
Weather Vane
Wheel of Chance

Wheel of Fortune
White House Steps
Wild Rose Wreath
Winding Ways
Winter Quilt
Wonder of the World
World Without End
Wreath and Star
Wreath of Grapes
Wreath of Roses

CHAPTER 6

APPENDIX

GLOSSARY

All-Over Set: includes patterns that use geometric pieces such as diamonds or hexagons across the total quilt top.

aniline dye: any of a large number of synthetic dyes derived from aniline, a colorless, oily, slightly water-soluble liquid usually derived from coal tar.

appliqué: a cutout design sewn onto or otherwise placed on a piece of material (such as a quilt top) as ornamentation.

asymmetrical: also called split blocks; the optical effect changes when the blocks are turned.

autograph quilt: a quilt in which each block is signed by a friend, usually with a poem, picture, or Bible verse.

backing: material attached to the back part of a quilt to support, strengthen, and protect it.

batting: cotton, wool, or synthetic fibers used as the middle layer of a quilt.

bees: gatherings of quilt makers to stitch finished tops; at first families were involved, later only quilt makers.

binding: fabric used to finish the raw outside edges of the quilt sandwich.

bleeding: color loss from washing.

block (of quilt): one section of patchwork on a quilt top, usually square.

block printing: method of printed patterns on fabric. A color dye is applied to the raised surface of a carved decorated wooden block, which is then placed on the fabric and hit lightly with a

block set: quilts made up of individual units, either pierced, appliquéd, plain, or embroidered, that are sewn together with or without sashing.

border: the fabric frame added around the outside of the patchwork top. Can be plain strips of fabric, pieced, or appliqué.

bridal quilt: the thirteenth in a Colonial girl's bakers dozen of quilts she took with her in marriage; not started until she was betrothed.

broadcloth: so named because it was woven wider than other fabrics, anywhere from 54 to 63 inches.

broderie-perse: a French term which literally translates as Persian embroidery. In quilt making it refers to the application (appliqué) of pictures or design motif cut from printed fabric onto a plain background style. In American quilts often a central medallion was used and embroidered.

calendar: a process using heat and rollers to glaze wool.

calico: small-scale-printed cotton fabric commonly used on quilts, usually floral in design, and created with the roller press printing technique.

central medallion: early quilt design of European origins, where a single image dominates the field of the quilt top; can be done in appliquéd or pieced form.

challis: a soft wool or wool-and-cotton cloth; plain, printed, or figured, and unglazed; twill weave.

chambray: a gingham-type fabric, plain weave, often with a colored warp and a white weft.

cheater cloth: fabric printed with patchwork designs that look like completed blocks.

cherryderrys: a fabric with silk warp and cotton weft from the 1750s.

coal tar: the residue created when coal is heated in a closed container in the absence of air and the most important component of all synthetic dyes.

colorfastness: when a dye doesn't bleed, or fade, when it's washed.

color loss: when fabrics fade or change color from washing, inferior dyes, exposure to light, crocking.

comforter: three layers—a fabric top, usually whole-cloth, sometimes pieced; a batting; and a backing—held together by knots tied with thread or yarn.

commemorative quilts: made to record a special event in history.

compactness: how tightly a fabric is woven; the more threads per square inch, the more compact the weave.

conversational or object prints: miniature prints, excluding floral designs but including insects, animals, sporting motifs, etc., done on the roller press.

copper cylinder: a design is cut into copper, but instead of pressing the cylinder on a fabric, the fabric is rolled under the cylinder to print it.

copperplate printing: eighteenth-century technique where dye or mordant is placed over an etched, engraved, or pattern-incised copper plate, which leaves dye in the grooves to be transferred to fabric.

corded work: two layers of fabric held together by close, parallel lines of running or back stitching that make a predetermined design. It involves a large-eyed needle threaded with soft cording that is inserted from the back and pulled thru the design outlines. The result is a raised look.

counterpane: any bed cover, often but not necessarily a quilt.

coverlet: any bedspread or bed covering used chiefly for warmth, not necessarily a quilt.

cretonne: a nineteenth-century large-scale-printed fabric very similar to chintz and frequently used for furnishings or quilt backings.

crocking: when a fabric loses color from its surface.

dimity: a thin, white, dyed, or printed cotton fabric woven with a stripe or check of heavier yarn.

direct or substantive dyes: a natural dye derived from organic matter.

discharge printing: a method of fabric printing in which the material is dyed and then certain areas are "discharged" with a solution that permits the original hue or its color replacement to act as a pattern against the colored ground.

eccentric prints: a geometric-patterned fabric first created by an error in which a roller press jammed on a striped fabric, producing jagged angles and optical illusions of three dimensions.

embroidery: needlework using silk, wool, or cotton thread in decorative stitches.

face: the side of the material meant to be seen.

field: the open spaces on a quilt top extending from the center out toward all four edges and corners.

friendship quilts or blocks: quilts of blocks made by more than one quilt maker or, if made by one quilt maker, given to memorialize a friendship.

fugitive: changing color when exposed to light and chemical substances produced in the atmosphere, in other pigments, or in the medium.

geometric: refers to squares, triangles, diamonds, and other straight-lined shapes; usually refers to pieced quilts, especially those with optical illusion effects.

gingham: cotton fabric, originally from nineteenth-century Scotland, of at least two colors woven into checks or stripes.

glaze: an additive to make fabric stiffer and appear shiny.

grogrinetts: a worsted with watermarks.

homespun: cloth hand-woven from home-grown wool, cotton, or flax by Colonial and pioneer households.

indigo dye: natural blue dye derived from the indigo plant.

linsey-woolsey: a fabric made using two threads, one from wool and one from linen.

loft: the puffiness on a quilt top from the batting beneath.

madder dye: reddish color produced by a flowering plant that grows in Europe. A term used to describe the reddish, deep browns used in quilts in the middle 1800s.

microwaving: a method of artificially aging fabric.

mordant: metallic compound or salt (such as oxide) used with natural dyes to make them colorfast.

motif: a totally recognizable element of a design: for example, a floral motif.

mourning print: white cotton fabric printed with fine black lines in any of a variety of designs, circa 1890-1925.

multigenerational quilt: any quilt worked on by different quilt makers of different generations.

muslin: a fine cotton fabric first made in India.

natural dye: a dye extracted from organic matter.

nine-patch: the most frequently used division in geometric pieced blocks. The basic block is broken into three rows of three squares each, making nine segments that could be further divided.

one-patch: when the same single shape—such as hexagons, tumblers, and triangles—is used to create an entire quilt top.

patchwork: the process of assembling smaller pieces of cloth together to make a quilt top.

pieced (quilt): made by, or as if by, joining pieced segments together to form an enlarged top.

penciling or brush dyeing: an overdyeing process done by hand.

quilt: a sandwich of three layers: a top, usually of patchwork but sometimes whole-cloth; a batting; and a backing fabric.

quilt frame: four long boards with clamps used to hold the quilt sandwich tight while stitching.

quilt kits: packaged, pre-cut, pre-designed quilt materials and directions.

quilting: the stitching that holds the quilt sandwich together.

rainbow print: fabric style with different color and shading intensity, created on the roller press and using graduated amounts of dye, circa 1825-1840.

resist technique: printing method using waxes or pastes to control areas not intended for dyeing.

reverse appliqué: the method of placing two fabrics together, cutting out the top fabric so the back fabric shows thru, and then turning under and stitching down the raw edges.

roller printing: method of printing using an engraved copper plate fashioned into cylindrical form and used to decorate continuous rolls of material.

sashing: strips of fabric sewn between quilt blocks, joining them to create a quilt top. Sashing strips may use both appliquéd and pieced designs.

satin weave: where each weft yarn passes over several warps and "floats," producing a surface sheen.

scrap bag: the accumulation of pieces of fabric saved from other needlework or other quilts that are too small to use for clothing but too big to be thrown out.

selvage: the warp edges of a textile which are finished to prevent fraying.

set: the way the blocks are assembled in the top. Straight set puts the blocks in horizontal and vertical rows. Blocks set on point appear as diamond shapes in a quilt top.

staple: the fibers, of animal or vegetable origin, used to make thread.

stipple quilting: when tiny stitches are sewed in close rows to create a higher loft in unquilted areas.

stuffed work (also called white work): stitching method popular in the eighteenth and early nineteenth centuries in which two fabrics are quilted together to create a sculptured design, effected by small stitches in intricate designs and stuffed loosely from the back, usually with woven homespun. This produced highlights and shadows in the quilt design.

symmetrical blocks: those geometric pieced patterns that always form the same design no matter how they're assembled.

tea-dyeing: an artificial method of aging fabric;

sometimes used to make new fabrics blend in with old, sometimes used to make a new quilt appear as an antique.

template: fabric basted over paper patterns, and each piece is then whipstitched together to form an allover design. Most often used for diamond and hexagon form patterns.

tendering: when fabric wears out. Many times caused by the harsh mordant and resist chemicals used to fix dyes.

trapunto: similar to stuffed work, but not stuffed from the back, rather incorporating the batting of the quilt.

tufting: method of joining together the layers of a quilt by pulling lengths of cord, yarn, etc. up from the back and knotting them off in the front.

vat process: a dyeing technique that requires an alkaline vat along with oxidation to induce the dye to dissolve in water and remain colorfast.

velvet: a pile fabric made of silk, wool, or cotton fibers.

warp: the set of yarns placed lengthwise in the loom, crossed and interlaced with the weft, and forming the lengthwise threads in a woven fashion.

weft: the set of yarns going in a horizontal direction, going from selvage to selvage; crosswise.

whitework: the design of these quilts is solely from the quilting pattern; usually done with whole-cloth although newer quilts may use plain colored fabric.

whole-cloth: quilts in which the tops are not patchwork but a single piece of fabric.

wood-block printing: a method in which patterns are added to cloth by using wood blocks cut into designs. Either dye or mordants were pressed onto the cloth.

Museums

American Quilter's Society Quilt Museum
214 Jefferson Street
Paducah, KY 42001
502-442-8856

The Cooper Hewitt Museum
2 East 92nd Street
New York, NY 10128
212-860-6868

The Detroit Institute of Arts
5200 Woodward Avenue
Detroit, MI 48202
313-833-7900

Esprit
900 Minnesota Street
San Francisco, CA 94105
415-648-6900

Hennepin County Historical Society Museum
2303 Third Avenue South
Minneapolis, MN 55404
612-870-1329

The Henry Ford Museum and Greenwich Village
20900 Oakwood Boulevard
Dearborn, MI 48121
313-271-1620

The Kalona Quilt and Textile Museum
413 $^1/_2$ "B" Avenue
Kalona, IA 52247
319-656-2240

The Milwaukee Public Museum
800 West Wells Street
Milwaukee, WI 53233
414-278-2720

The Mount Vernon Ladies Association
Mount Vernon, VA 22121
703-780-2000

Museum of American Folk Art
2 Lincoln Square
New York, NY 10023
212-595-9533

Old Sturbridge Village
Sturbridge, MA 01566
617-347-3362

The Rocky Mountain Quilt Museum
1111 Washington Street
Golden, CO 80401
303-277-0377

The Shelburne Museum
Route 7
Shelburne, VT 05482
802-985-3346

The Textile Museum
2320 S. Street NW
Washington, DC 20008
202-667-0441

The Witte Museum
3801 Broadway
San Antonio, TX 78209
512-829-7262

SOURCES AND RESOURCES

Alabama
Letha Sheppard
Route 1, Box 326
Wedowee, AL 36278

Arizona
Elaine Stonebraker
Via de Mañana
Scottsdale, AZ 85258
602-991-4144

Arkansas
Arkansas Country Quilts
Route 2, Box 31CC
Lexa, AR 72355
501-572-5820

California
Ames Gallery of American Folk Art
2661 Cedar Berkley
San Francisco, CA 94102
415-845-4949

Golyesther
7957 Melrose Avenue
Los Angeles, CA 90046
213-655-3393

The Great American Collective
1736 Lombard Street
San Francisco, CA 94123
415-922-2660

Hearts and Hands Galleries
241 Sir Francis Drake Blvd.
San Anselmo, CA 94960
415-453-7942

Margaret Cavigga Quilt Collection
8648 Melrose Avenue
Los Angeles, CA 90069
213-659-3020

Yankee Doodle Dandy
1974 Union Street
San Francisco, CA 94123
415-346-0346

Connecticut
The Connecticut Quilt Collection at Main Street Cellars Antiques
120 Main Street
New Canaan, CT 06840
203-966-8348

Pinney Street Antiques
50 Pinney Street
Ellington, CT 06029
203-871-1406

Susan Harris Amish Quilts
South Bald Hill Road
New Canaan, CT 06840
203-972-1424

Florida
Kavanagh's Antiques *(by appointment)*
6932 Willow Lane
Miami Lakes, FL 33014-2660
(954 or 305) 410-2596

Marge's Antiques
Stuart, FL
407-692-0188

Illinois
Illinois Artisan Shop
State of Illinois Center
100 W. Racine
Chicago, IL 60601
312-814-5321

Vale Craft Gallery
230 W. Superior
Chicago, IL 6060
Fax 312-337-3530

Wild Goose Chase Quilt Gallery
1511 Chicago Avenue
Evanston, IL 60210
708-328-1808

Indiana
Josephine Schepere
8057 East State Road 164
Celestina, IN 47521
812-389-2679

Iowa
The Woodin Wheel
515 "B" Avenue
Kalona, IA 52247
319-656-2240

Kentucky
Betty Upchurch
HC86, Box 25E
Monticello, KY 42633
606-348-9698

Massachusetts
**Calico Country: Antique Quilts and
Country Furnishings**
79 Washington Street
Marblehead, MA 01945
413-586-5853

The Cooperage
South Street and Route 119
P.O. Box 998
Townsend, MA 01469-0998
508-597-3042

Michael James
258 Old Colony Avenue
Somerset Village, MA 02726
508-672-1370

The Quilt Loft at Jos. Kilbridge Antiques
134 Main Street
Groton, MA 01450
508-468-3841

Rocky Mountain Quilts
248 East Main Street
Gloucester, MA 01930
508-281-3686

New Hampshire
Keepsake Quilting
Dover Street, P.O. Box 1459
Centre Harbor, NH 03253
603-279-3351

New York
Laura Fisher Antique Quilts and Americana
Gallery #57
1050 Second Avenue at 55th Street
New York, NY 10022
212-838-2596

Samuel Meier
Antique Textiles
328 East 59th Street, Suite 4
New York, NY 10022
212-644-8590

Betsy Brower
P.O. Box 831, Route 17M
Goshen, NY 10924
914-294-9420

Down Quilt Shop
518 Columbus Avenue
New York, NY 10024
212-496-8980

Hilltop Antiques
RD 2, Mekeel Street
Katonah, NY 10536
914-962-7272

Susan Parrish Antiques
390 Bleecker Street
New York, NY 10014
212-645-5020

North Carolina
Black Mountain Antiques
100 Sutton Avenue
Black Mountain, NC 28711
704-669-6218

The Country Peddler
West Main Street
Burnsville, NC 28714
704-682-7810

Ohio
Dairy Barn Southeastern Ohio Cultural Arts Center
P.O. Box 747
Athens, OH 45701-0747
Tel: 614-592-4981   Fax: 614-592-5090

Nancy Crow
P.O. Box 37
Baltimore, OH 43105
614-862-6554

Oregon
Ginnie Christie Quilts
38996 NE Scravel Hill Road
Albany, OR 97321
503-327-1473

Pennsylvania
Amish Country Traditions
The Fish Family
Strasburg Pike
Lancaster, PA 17602
717-687-9270

M. Finkel & Daughter
936 Pine Street
Philadelphia, PA 19107
215-627-7797

Omar & Sylvia Petersheim Quilts & Crafts
2544 Old Philadelphia Pike
Bird-in-Hand, PA 17505
717-392-6404

Pieces of the Heart
158 Shawnee Avenue
Easton, PA 18042
215-252-3673

Tennessee
Bets Ramsey
P.O. Box 4146
Chattanooga, TN 37405
615-265-4300

Wisconsin
**Quilts & Quilting,
Sandy & Ron Mason**
607 West Main Street
Princeton, WI 54968-0362
414-295-6506

SOURCES FOR MATERIALS FOR RESTORING

Process Materials
30 Veterans Boulevard
Rutherford, NJ 07070
201-935-2900

TALAS, Division of Technical Library Services
213 West 35th Street
New York, NY 10001
212-736-7744

University Products, Inc.
South Canal Street
Holyoke, MA 01041
413-532-9431

RESTORATION / CONSERVATION

Textile Conservators

Maury L. Bynum, P.E.
By Appointment
Tel: 312-474-WARP
    800-447-WARP
311 North Desplaines Street
Suite 601
Chicago, IL 60661

Robin Greeson Textile Restoration
Box 276, Snydertown Road
Craryville, NY 12521
518-851-7979

K & K Quilted
Box 23, Route 23
Hillsdale, NY 12529
518-325-4502

M. Finkel and Daughter
936 Pine Street
Philadelphia, PA 19107
215-627-7797

SOURCES AND RESOURCES

A major influence on contemporary quilt making is Quilts, Inc. It has been the parent corporation of International Quilt Festival since 1975; International Quilt market since 1979; Quilt Expo since 1988; and European Quilt market since 1988.

Organizations Affiliated with Quilts, Inc.

The Alliance for American Quilts
The Alliance is a non-profit entity founded by Karey Bresenhan, Nancy O'Bryant, Shelly Zegart, and Eunice Ray. The Alliance serves as an umbrella organization under which all elements of the quilt world may unite to achieve a permanent position for quilts as an art form, to preserve the history of quilting in women's lives, and to establish a place for future study and appreciation of quilts. The Alliance is developing the American Quilt Research Center and the International Quilt Index.

American International Quilt Association
AIQA is the only non-profit, international quilt association in the world. It was founded by Karey Bresenhan, Nancy O'Bryant, and their mothers, Jewel Patterson and Helen O'Bryant. AIQA is dedicated to the preservation

of the art of quilting, the attainment of public recognition for quilting as an art form, and the advancement of the state of the art thruout the world. It sponsors an annual judged show at International Quilt Festival, and supports a Grant Program that funds research and other quilt-related projects. Membership is worldwide and all members receive AIQA's quarterly journal, *Quilts...A World of Beauty.*

The Victoria Society

The Society is an outgrowth of A Victorian Romance®. It was established to communicate with members interested in Victoriana and a more serene lifestyle. The Society is a membership organization for those who are enchanted by the ambiance and elegance of the age of Queen Victoria and who aspire to incorporating "the essence of a gentler, more romantic era" into their homes and lives. For $35 a year members receive quarterly newsletters as well as various enhancements.

SHOWS PRODUCED BY QUILTS, INC.

Embellishment®

This consumer show premiered February 1995 in Austin, Texas, sponsored by *BEAD & Button* magazine. It spotlights the variety of beads, buttons, and other embellishments used in jewelry, on clothing, quilts, and other textile arts.

European Quilt Market

The only international trade show held in Europe for the quilting and soft crafts industry which takes place annually in a different European city.

International Quilt Festival

Largest annual quilt convention, show, sale, and Festival Quilt Making Academy in the world which takes place annually in Houston, Texas.

International Quilt Market

This market showcases quilting supplies, fabrics, decorative crafts, textile art, needle crafts, art apparel, and doll-making supplies for more than 15 years. It is the only wholesale trade show in the world for the quilting and soft crafts industry. IQM holds two shows a year in the United States and one a year in Europe.

Quilt Expo

The only international consumer show for the quilting public and quilting retailers doing business in Europe, is held in even numbered years following the European edition of International Quilt Market. Expos have been held in Salzburg, Austria; Odense, Denmark; The Hague, The Netherlands; and Karlsruhe, Germany.

A Victorian Romance®

A consumer show begun in February 1993 that focuses on the romantic aspects of that era—potpourri, afternoon tea, lace and linens, collections of all sorts, hearts, silver teapots, Crazy quilts, and more. It features special exhibits, lanes of unique boutiques, lectures, demonstrations, and other special events.

1. What are three of the most important ways to date a quilt?

2. If a quilt is said to be made of "cheater cloth" what does that mean?

3. There have been many revivals and new patterns introduced over the years, but what was the most significant change in quilting and when did it occur?

4. What country has been (and still does) reproducing historical quilt patterns?

5. When a quilt has a change within the pattern, or is missing a piece in the design, should you pass it up?

6. How can you tell if a quilt is "Amish"?

7. What is the first thing you do when considering the purchase of an "old" quilt?

8. Why are some quilts referred to as "Log Cabin"?

9. How is a "Crazy Quilt" put together?

10. Some patterns have more than one name. Can you give an example?

11. What are the most expensive quilt types?

12. Name the most popular quilt pattern.

13. When was the color purple first used in quilts?

CHAPTER 7

14. What was a "quilting Bee" and its function?

15. How can you tell if a quilt has new replacements?

16. What is the proper way to store a quilt?

17. Describe a "Yo-Yo" quilt.

18. What type of quilts are popular to hang on the wall?

19. When you buy a quilt what should you ask the seller for?

20. What is the difference between "pieced" and "patchwork"?

Answers

1. *Fabric, colors and patterns.*

2. *Cloth printed with old quilt designs.*

3. *The "Art Quilt" using a variety of techniques, mixed media, 1970s.*

4. *China.*

5. *No. This was intentionally done by the quilter. It can add to the value and interest.*

6. *Boldly colored in geometric patterns.*

7. *Count the number of stitches per inch. More, the better.*

8. *Their blocks resemble log cabin logs.*

9. *A mix of unrelated fabrics, colors, stitches, motifs usually pieced on the foundation.*

10. *"Drunkard's Path" also known as World's Puzzle, etc.*

11. *Baltimore Album quilts signed or attributed to specific maker, early Amish and crib quilts.*

12. *The Double-Wedding Ring.*

13. *Around the Civil War.*

14. *A combination social, learning experience and quilters working together to finish a single or more, quilt.*

15. *Difference in number of stitches in an area, new binding or borders.*

16. *Either wrapped in cotton cloth or rolled with acid-free products.*

17. *Fabric circles gathered, fastened then stitched together to simulate a Yo-Yo motif.*

18. *Old quilts with bold, colorful designs or contemporary Art quilts.*

19. *Documentation of when and where the quilt was made, etc.*

20. *Patchwork is the putting together of many pieces of fabric, cut in patches, blocks or other designs. Piecing is the end result when they are stitched to form a total pattern, and a finished quilt.*

BIBLIOGRAPHY

Allen, Gloria Seaman. *Old Line Traditions: Maryland Women and Their Quilts*. Washington, D.C.: D.A.R. Museum, 1985.

Allen, Gloria Seaman and Nancy Gibson Tuckhorn. *A Maryland Album: Quiltmaking Traditions 1634-1934*. Nashville, Tennessee: Rutledge Hill Press, 1995.

"American Women's Gift to France." *Harper's Bazaar*. Vol. 53, No. 20 (May 19, 1900): 151.

An American Sampler: Folk Art from the Shelburne Museum. Washington, D.C.: National Gallery of Art, 1987.

Atkins, Jacqueline M., ed. *Discover America and Friends Sharing America*. New York: Dutton Studio Books in association with the Museum of American Folk Art, 1991.

Atkins, Jacqueline M., ed. *Memories of Childhood*. New York: E.P. Dutton in association with the Museum of American Folk Art, 1989.

Atkins, Jacqueline M. and Phyllis A. Tepper. *New York Beauties: Quilts from the Empire State*. New York: Dutton Studio Books in association with the Museum of American Folk Art, 1992.

Atkins, Jacqueline M. *Shared Threads: Quilting Together—Past and Present*. New York: Viking Studio Books in association with the Museum of American Folk Art, 1994.

Benberry, Cuesta. *Always There: The African-American Presence in American Quilts*. Louisville, Kentucky: The Kentucky Quilt Project, Inc., 1992.

Benberry, Cuesta. "The 20th Century's First Quilt Revival, Part I: The Interim Period." *Quilter's Newsletter Magazine*. Vol. 10, No. 7 (July-August 1979): 20-22.

Benberry, Cuesta. "The 20th Century's First Quilt Revival, Part II: The First Quilt Revival." *Quilter's Newsletter Magazine*. Vol. 10, No. 8 (September 1979): 25-26; 29.

Benberry, Cuesta. "The 20th Century's First Quilt Revival, Part III: The World War I Era." *Quilter's Newsletter Magazine*. Vol. 10, No. 9 (October 1979): 10-11, 37.

Benberry, Cuesta. "Afro-American Women and Quilts." *Uncoverings—Research Papers of the American Quilt Study Group* (1980): 64-67.

Bishop, Robert and Carter Houck. *All Flags Flying: American Patriotic Quilts as Expressions of Liberty.* New York: E.P. Dutton in association with The Museum of American Folk Art, 1986.

Bishop, Robert. *The Romance of Double Wedding Ring Quilts.* New York: E.P. Dutton in association with The Museum of American Folk Art, 1989.

Bowman, Doris M. *The Smithsonian Treasury: American Quilts.* Washington, D.C.: Smithsonian Press, 1991.

Brackman, Barbara. "Blue-and-White Quilts." *Quilter's Newsletter Magazine.* Vol. 18, No. 3 (March, 1987): 22-26.

Brackman, Barbara. *Clues in the Calico: A Guide to Identifying and Dating Antique Quilts.* McLean, Virginia: EPM Publications, Inc., 1989.

Brackman, Barbara. *Encyclopedia of Appliqué: An Illustrated, Numerical Index to Traditional and Modern Patterns.* McLean, Virginia: EPM Publications, Inc., 1993.

Brackman, Barbara. *Encyclopedia of Pieced Quilt Patterns.* Paducah, Kentucky: American Quilter's Society, 1993.

Brackman, Barbara. "Fairs and Expositions: Their Influence on American Quilts." *Bits and Pieces: Textile Traditions.* Lewisburg, Pennsylvania: Oral Traditions Project of the Union County Historical Society, 1991:90-99.

Brackman, Barbara. "The Strip Tradition in European-American Quilts." *The Clarion.* Vol. 14, No. 4 (Fall 1989): 44-51.

Brackman, Barbara. "Signature Quilts: Nineteenth Century Trends." *Uncoverings.* Vol. 10 (1989): 25-37.

Bresenhan, Karoline Patterson and Nancy O'Bryant Puentes. *Lone Stars: A Legacy of Texas Quilts, 1836-1936.* Austin, Texas: University of Texas Press, 1986.

Brooks, Marilyn, ed. *The World of Quilts At Meadowbrook Hall.* Rochester, Michigan: Oakland University, 1983.

Bullard, Lacy Folmar and Betty Joe Shiell. *Chintz Quilts: Unfading Glory.* Tallahassee, Florida: Serendipity Press, 1983.

Caulfield, Sophia Frances Anne and Blanche C. Saward. *The Dictionary of Needlework: An Encyclopedia of Artistic, Plain, and Fancy Needlework.* London: A.W. Cowan, 1882. Reprint, *Encyclopedia of Victorian Needlework.* New York: Dover Publications, Inc., 1972.

Christopherson, Katy. *The Political and Campaign Quilt.* Frankfort, Kentucky: The Kentucky Heritage Quilt Society, 1984.

Clark, Ricky. *Quilted Gardens: Floral Quilts of the Nineteenth Century.* Nashville, Tennessee: Rutledge Hill Press, 1994.

Collins, Herbert Ridgeway. *Threads of History: Americana Recorded on Cloth, 1775 to the Present.* Washington, D.C.: Smithsonian Institution, 1979.

Clarke, Bea Fleming. Interview. Tallahassee, Fla., May 11, 1989.

Crow, Nancy. *Quilts and Influences.* Paducah, KY: American Quilter's Society, 1990.

Douglas, Marjory Stoneman. *Florida: The Long Frontier.* New York: Harper and Row, 1967.

Duke, Dennis and Deborah Harding, eds. *America's Glorious Quilts.* New York: Hugh Lauter Levin Associates, Inc., 1987.

Ferrero, Pat, Elaine Hedges, and Julie Silber. *Hearts and Hands: The Influence of Women and Quilts on American Society.* San Francisco: The Quilt Digest Press, 1987.

Finley, Ruth E. *Old Patchwork Quilts and The Women Who Made Them.* Philadelphia and London: J.B. Lippincott, 1929. Reprint, Newton Centre, Massachusetts: Charles T. Branford, 1957.

Fox, Sandi. *Wrapped in Glory: Figurative Quilts and Bedcovers 1700–1900.* New York: Thames and Hudson, Inc. and The Los Angeles County Museum of Art, 1990.

Fox, Sandi. "Comments from the Quilt," *Modern Maturity*, Vol. 33, No. 4, Aug/Sep 1990, p. 58-63.

Gale Research Company. *Currier & Ives: A Catalogue Raisonne.* Detroit: Gale Research, 1983.

Garoutte, Sally. "Marseilles Quilts and Their Woven Offspring." *Uncoverings.* Vol. 3 (1982): 115-134.

Godey's Lady's Book. Philadelphia: Louis A. Godey, January 1835.

Goldsborough, Jennifer Faulds. *Lavish Legacies: Baltimore Album and Related Quilts in the Collection of the Maryland Historical Society.* Baltimore, Maryland: Maryland Historical Society, 1994.

Goldsborough, Jennifer F. "An Album of Baltimore Album Quilt Studies." *Uncoverings.* Vol. 15 (1994): 73-110.

Goldsborough, Jennifer F. "Baltimore Album Quilts." *The Magazine Antiques.* Vol. CXLV, No. 3 (March 1994): 412-421.

Granick, Eve Wheatcroft. *The Amish Quilt.* Intercourse, Pennsylvania: Good Books, 1989.

Groves, Harold and Dorothymae Groves, eds. *Kansas City Star Classic Quilt Patterns: Motifs and Design*. Kansas City, Missouri: Groves Publishing Company, 1988.

Gunn, Virginia. "Crazy Quilts and Outline Quilts: Popular Responses to the Decorative Art / Art Needlework Movement, 1876–1893." *Uncoverings*. Vol. 5 (1984): 131-152.

Gunn, Virginia. "Dress Fabrics of the Late 19th Century: Their Relationships to Period Quilts." *Bits and Pieces: Textiles Traditions*. Lewisburg, Pennsylvania: Oral Traditions Project of the Union County Historical Society, 1991: 4-15.

Gunn, Virginia. "Victorian Silk Template Patchwork in American Periodicals 1850–1875." *Uncoverings*. Vol. 4 (1983): 9-25.

Hall, Carrie A. and Rose G. Kretsinger. *The Romance of the Patchwork Quilt in America*. Caldwell, Idaho: Caxton Printers Ltd., 1935. Reprint, New York: Dover, 1988.

Hollander, Stacy C. "African-American Quilts: Two Perspectives." *Folk Art Magazine of the Museum of American Folk Art*. Vol. 18, No. 1 (Spring 1993): 44-51.

Holstein, Jonathan. *The Pieced Quilt: An American Design Tradition*. Boston, Massachusetts: New York Graphic Society, 1973.

Hostetler, John A. *Amish Society*, Third Edition. Baltimore and London: The Johns Hopkins University Press, 1980.

Johnson, Allen and Dumas Malone, eds. *Dictionary of American Biography*. Vol. VI. New York: Charles Scribner's Sons, 1931.

Johnson, Mary Elizabeth. *Star Quilts*. New York: Clarkson N. Potter, 1992.

Katzenberg, Dena S. *Baltimore Album Quilts*. Baltimore: The Baltimore Museum of Art, 1981.

Kaufman, Stanley A. with Leroy Beachy. *Amish in Eastern Ohio*. Walnut Creek, Ohio: Ohio Arts Council, 1990.

Kiracofe, Roderick and Mary Elizabeth Johnson. *The American Quilt: A History of Cloth and Comfort 1750–1950*. New York: Clarkson N. Potter, 1993.

Kogan, Lee. "The Quilt Legacy of Elizabeth, New Jersey." *The Clarion*. Vol. 15, No. 1 (Winter 1990): 58-64.

Lasansky, Jeannette, ed. *Pieced by Mother: Over 100 Years of Quiltmaking Traditions*. Lewisburg, Pennsylvania: Union County Historical Society, 1987.

Lasansky, Jeannette. "Quilts of Central Pennsylvania." *The Magazine Antiques*. Vol. CXXXI, No. 1 (January 1987): 288-299.

Lasansky, Jeannette. "The Typical Versus the Unusual / Distortions of Time." *In the Heart of Pennsylvania: Symposium Papers*. Lewisburg, Pennsylvania: Oral Traditions Project of the Union County Historical Society, 1986: 56–63.

Laury, Jean Ray. *Imagery on Fabric*. Lafayette, CA; C & T Publishing, 1992.

Laverty, Paula. "Many Hands: The Story of an Album Quilt." *Folk Art: Magazine of the Museum of American Folk Art*. Vol. 18, No. 1 (Spring 1993): 52-57.

Lynn, Catherine. "Decorating Surfaces: Aesthetic Delight, Theoretical Dilemma." *In Pursuit of Beauty*. New York: The Metropolitan Museum of Art and Rizzoli, 1986.

Lynn, Catherine. "Surface Ornament: Wallpapers, Carpets, Textiles and Embroidery." *In Pursuit of Beauty*. New York: The Metropolitan Museum of Art and Rizzoli, 1986.

Mathieson, Judy. "Some Published Sources of Design Inspiration for the Quilt Pattern Mariner's Compass—17th to 20th Century." *Uncoverings* (1981): 11-18.

McCloskey, Marsha. *Feathered Star Quilts*. Bothell, Washington: That Patchwork Place, 1987.

McKim, Ruby. *101 Patchwork Patterns*, 2nd ed. New York: Dover Publications, Inc. 1962.

McMorris, Penny. *Crazy Quilts*. New York: E.P. Dutton, Inc., 1984.

McMorris, Penny and Michael Kile. *The Art Quilt*. San Francisco: The Quilt Digest Press, 1986.

James, Michael: *The Quiltmaker's Handbook: A Guide to Design and Construction*. Englewood Cliffs, NJ: Prentice-Hall.

Montgomery, Florence M. *Printed Textiles: English and American Cottons and Linens 1700–1850*. New York: Viking Press, 1970.

Montgomery, Florence M. *Textiles in America, 1650–1870*. New York: W.W. Norton, 1984.

Needle-Craft: Artistic and Practical. New York: The Butterick Publishing Co., 1889.

Needle and Brush: Useful and Decorative. New York: The Butterick Publishing Co., 1889.

Pellman, Rachel T. and Joanne Ranck. *Quilts Among the Plain People*. Intercourse, PA: Good Books, 1981. People's Place Booklet No. 4.

Pierce, Sue and Verna Suit. *Art Quilts: Playing with a Full Deck*. San Francisco: Pomegranate Artbooks, 1994.

Pottinger, David. *Quilts from the Indiana Amish, A Regional Collection*. New York: E.P. Dutton and Co. in association with the Museum of American Folk Art, 1983.

Puentes, Nancy O'Bryant. *First Aid for Family Quilts*. Wheatridge, CO: Leman Publications, Inc., 1986. Their address for ordering is: Box 394-4 6700 West 44th Avenue, Wheatridge, CO 80034.

The Quilt Digest 1,2. San Francisco: Kiracofe and Kile, 1983-84.

The Quilt Digest 3-5. San Francisco: Quilt Digest Press, 1985–87.

Rae, Janet. *Quilts of the British Isles*. New York: E.P. Dutton, 1987.

Roan, Nancy and Donald Roan. *Lest I Shall Be Forgotten: Anecdotes and Traditions of Quilts*. Green Lane, Pennsylvania, Goschenhoppen Historians, Inc., 1993.

Safford, Carleton L. and Robert Bishop. *American's Quilts and Coverlets*. New York: E.P. Dutton and Co., 1985.

Schorsch, Anita. *Plain & Fancy: Country Quilts of the Pennsylvania-Germans*. New York: Sterling Publishing Co., Inc., 1992.

Sherman, Mimi. "A Fabric of One Family: A Saga of Discovery." *The Clarion*. Vol. 14, No. 2 (Spring 1989): 55-62.

Shirer, Marie. *The Quilters' How-To Dictionary*. Wheat Ridge, CO: Leman Publications, Inc., 1991.

Sienkiewicz, Eleanor Hamilton. "The Marketing of Mary Evans." *Uncoverings*. Vol. 10 (1989): 7-24.

Sudo, Kumiko. *Expressive Quilts*. Berkeley, CA: Pegasus Publishing, 1989.

"The Meetin' Place" (about Kumido Sudo). *Quilter's Newsletter Magazine*, Vol. 18, No. 6 (November-December 1897): 24.

Swan, Susan Burrows. *Plain & Fancy: American Women and Their Needlework, 1700–1850*. New York: Holt, Rinehart, and Winston, 1977.

Thieme, Otto Charles. "Wave High the Red Bandanna: Some Handkerchiefs of the 1888 Presidential Campaign." *Journal of American Culture*. Vol. 3, No. 4 (Winter 1980): 686-705.

Vincent, Margaret: *The Ladies' Work Table: Domestic Needlework in Nineteenth-Century America*. Allentown, PA: Allentown Art Museum, 1988.

Vlach John Michael. *The Afro-American Tradition in Decorative Arts*. Cleveland: Cleveland Museum of Art, 1978.

Wahlman, Maude Southwell, Ph.D. "African-American Quilts: Tracing the Aesthetic Principles." *The Clarion.* Vol. 14, No. 2 (Spring 1989): 44-54.

Wahlman, Maude Southwell, Ph.D. "Religious Symbolism in African-American Quilts." *The Clarion.* Vol. 14, No. 3 (Summer 1989): 36-44.

Wahlman, Maude Southwell, Ph.D. *Signs and Symbols: African Images in African-American Quilts.* New York: Studio Books in association with the Museum of American Folk Art, 1993.

Waldvogel, Merikay. *Soft Covers for Hard Times: Quiltmaking and the Great Depression.* Nashville, TN: Rutledge Hill Press, 1990.

Waldvogel, Merikay and Barbara Brackman. *Patchwork Souvenirs of the 1993 World's Fair.* Nashville, TN: Rutledge Hill Press, 1993.

Webster, Marie D. "The May Tulip Quilt in Appliqué." *Needlecraft: The Magazine of the Home Arts.* (May 1931): 6.

Webster, Marie D. *Quilts, Their Story and How to Make Them.* Garden City, New York: Tudor Publishing, 1948.

Wilder, Donna. "Quilts at an Exhibition." In *America's Glorious Quilts,* edited by Dennis Duke and Deborah Harding. New York: Hugh Lauter Levin Associates, Inc., 1987.

Woodard, Thos. K. and Blanche Greenstein. *Twentieth Century Quilts: 1900–1950.* New York: E.P. Dutton, Inc., 1988.

CATALOGS OF PAST QUILT NATIONAL EXHIBITIONS:

Quilts: The State of an Art / Quilt National. West Chester, PA: Schiffer Publishing Co., 1985.

Fiber Expressions: The Contemporary Quilt / Quilt National. West Chester, PA; Schiffer Publishing Co., 1987.

International Contemporary Quilt–Art Exhibition '88. Tokyo: The Cultural Project Department 1, Asahi Shimbun, 1988.

New Quilts: Interpretations & Innovations / Quilt National. West Chester, PA: Schiffer Publishing Co., 1989.